THE
STYLE
DIARIES

ALSO BY NEIL STRAUSS

The Game: Penetrating the Secret Society of Pickup Artists

How to Make Money Like a Porn Star

WITH BERNARD CHANG

The Long Hard Road Out of Hell

WITH MARILYN MANSON

The Dirt

WITH MÖTLEY CRÜE

How to Make Love Like a Porn Star

WITH JENNA JAMESON

Don't Try This at Home

WITH DAVE NAVARRO

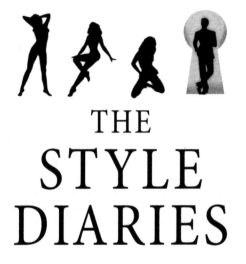

THE
STYLE
DIARIES

THE PICKUP ARTIST'S
COMPANION

Neil Strauss

HARPER

NEW YORK • LONDON • TORONTO • SYDNEY

HARPER

HarperCollins books may be purchased for educational, business, or sales promotional use. For information please write: Special Markets Department, HarperCollins Publishers, 10 East 53rd Street, New York, NY 10022.

Some names and distinguishing details have been changed to protect the identities of the debauched.

FIRST EDITION

Designed by Jaime Putorti
Interior Illustrations by Bernard Chang

Library of Congress Cataloging-in-Publication Data is available upon request.

ISBN: 978-0-06-154044-8
ISBN-10: 0-06-154044-7

07 08 09 10 11 DIX/IM 10 9 8 7 6 5 4 3 2 1

I here present you, courteous reader, with the record of a remarkable period in my life, according to my application of it. I trust that it will prove not merely an interesting record, but, in a considerable degree, useful and instructive. In *that* hope it is, that I have drawn it up: and *that* must be my apology for breaking through that delicate and honorable reserve, which, for the most part, restrains us from the public exposure of our own errors and infirmities. Nothing, indeed, is more revolting to English feelings, than the spectacle of a human being obtruding on our notice his moral ulcers or scars.

—THOMAS DE QUINCEY,
CONFESSIONS OF AN ENGLISH OPIUM-EATER, 1821

THE RULES OF THE GAME GOVERN OUR LIVES,
OUR PROSPERITY, AND OUR HAPPINESS.

THE RULES OF THE GAME ARE EMOTIONAL
AND NOT LOGICAL.

THE RULES OF THE GAME HAVE BEEN THE SAME
THROUGHOUT HUMAN HISTORY, REGARDLESS OF RACE,
CULTURE, OR NATIONALITY.

THE RULES OF THE GAME ARE IMMUTABLE.

THE RULES OF THE GAME CAN GET YOU LAID,
LOVED, MARRIED, IMMORTALIZED.

THEY CAN ALSO GET YOU BETRAYED, DUMPED,
DEPRESSED, STALKED, BEATEN, STABBED, SHOT.

HANDLE THEM WITH CARE—FOR THESE PAGES ARE
INTENDED NOT AS PRESCRIPTION
BUT RATHER AS PREVENTION.

CONTENTS

PREFACE

"What are your goals?" he asked.

"My goals?"

"Yeah. Unless you know where you're going, you won't know how to get there."

"I guess my goal is quantity, quality, and variety. My goal is to make out with women I just met, get blow jobs in club bathrooms, sleep with a different person every other night, and find myself in strange sexual adventures with multiple women."

He sat in silence, listening, so I continued. I'd never articulated it before, either out loud or to myself. This was several years ago, just after I had discovered the Rosetta Stone of attraction in the form of an underground society of master pickup artists. "I want to corrupt young virgins, reawaken passions in bored housewives, seduce and be seduced by stars, students, centerfolds, businesswomen, and Tantric goddesses. And then, from amongst these women, I will choose one to love."

"How will you know when you've found her?" he asked.

"I guess I'll just know, because I won't want to be with other women anymore."

"Well, that sounds like a good plan. And it makes sense to a point." I waited. I knew he was about to find the flaw in my logic. "But what happens after a year or two years, and the sex isn't as exciting anymore? What happens if you have a child with her, and she becomes less available for you emotionally and sexually? What happens if you go through a rough patch and start fighting all the time?"

"If those things happened, I'd probably want to sleep with other women." I watched him as he lifted his legs off the floor and crossed them on the couch in a position of spiritual superiority. "But I'd just have to control myself. I suppose I could think of other women like cigarettes. Even though I desired them, I would refrain from indulging because I'd know it was bad for the health of the relationship."

And then I waited for it, the inevitable question. He was a music producer, yet he never seemed to work. Instead, I'd meet him at his house in Malibu, and we'd spend hours discussing the meaning of life while his Indian houseboy brought us bottles of water and plates of vegan food.

"So," he said, "you'd be okay spending the next fifty years sleeping with only one woman?"

He had walked me into the weakness in my romantic strategy, and probably in most men's. I love women's laughter. I love their lips, their hips, their skin, their touch, the way their faces look when they're in the throes of sexual ecstasy. I love the way they nurture, feel, care, intuit, understand unconditionally. I yearn to create that bubble of passion, which draws us into the moment and connects us to the energy of the universe. And I cherish, more than anything, the moment in bed right after the first time, when all that there is to hold on to has been given. "Well, that would be difficult for me," I admitted. "Ideally, I'd like to be able to have my cake and eat it."

"I think that's a reasonable request," he said. "After all, cake was meant to be eaten. Who actually orders a cake, then doesn't touch it?"

"So what you're saying is that there's a way to be in a committed, loving relationship, yet still sleep with other women?"

"I didn't say that. All I said is that there's a way to have a cake and eat it."

"How? Even a monogamous relationship is a challenge. That's why twenty-five percent of all crimes are domestic violence, that's why the divorce rate is fifty percent, that's why the majority of men and women have cheated. Maybe the relationship paradigm that's been forced on us by society isn't natural." He looked at me disapprovingly. I continued anyway. "Even if you're faithful for those fifty years, you still may check out a woman walking by or leaf through a copy of *Maxim* or look for porn on the Internet one night. And this is going to make your partner feel like she's not enough for you."

"This is true. You can't have a healthy relationship if your partner doesn't feel secure."

"Exactly. So, considering the nature of men, how is it possible to make a woman feel secure in a relationship?"

"Probably by not wanting to have your cake and eat it," he said.

"But that's not natural. You just said that cake was meant to be eaten."

"Well, then," he said, "you'll have to find a way to eat it without hurting someone you love."

I hated him sometimes. For being right.

In the days that followed, I sifted through the conversation in my mind, searching for answers. I talked to men and women everywhere I went, asking each the same question: "If you didn't have to worry about having children and you didn't need someone to take care of you when you were older, would you still get married?"

Most men said no. Most women said yes. And that was when I realized that the traditional relationship model is defined by a woman's needs, not a man's.

Then I started asking a new question:

"Let's say you met someone, clicked on every level, and wanted to date this person. But the person said that after two years, he or she would disappear from your life forever and there was nothing you could do about it. Would you still date this person?"

Most women said no. Most men said yes—some even said the scenario would be ideal.

So where does that leave the "one woman, one man, happily ever after" myth that is the basis of our entire civilization? Apparently, on an unbalanced scale, because the natural instincts of men seem to be to alternate between periods of love relationships and periods of hedonistic bachelorhood, with some traumatized kids thrown in as an evolutionary imperative.

When I next met my friend, I shared my conclusion. "That's kind of a sad way to live one's life," he said.

"Yeah, and the problem is that's exactly how I've been living mine. Except for the kids part. I don't want to traumatize them, so I'm waiting until I figure out a solution to this whole relationship dilemma that satisfies the needs of both sexes."

"You'd make a good politician," he said, not as a compliment.

"You're the type of guy who can't kill a fly, a bee, or a cockroach himself, but has no problem hiring an exterminator to kill a whole swarm of them."

"What's that supposed to mean?"

"It means," he said, setting down his bottle of water, "that your ethics are fucked up."

We live in a society that likes to make clear-cut judgments—between good and bad, right and wrong, successful and unsuccessful. But that is not how the universe works. The universe does not judge. Since the dawn of time, it has operated on just two principles: the creative and the destructive. We have come to terms with the creative impulse—that, after all, is why we're here—but we live in fear of the destructive because that, one day, will be our reason for going.

I don't want to just offer you a self-help book and tell you that, if you follow it, in thirty days your life will be perfect. There's another side to the game: the destructive side. And, the more successful you are, the more you're going to rub against it. Especially since, more than any other instinct we have, the sexual impulse contains both the creative and the destructive.

The inspiration for this book was the preceding series of conversations, which point to a seemingly irreconcilable disparity between the sexual and emotional needs of men and women—not to mention a reluctance to admit and express them. They also underscore a similarity that transcends gender: the fear of being alone—and the dramas and comedies that occur because, as the director Rainer Werner Fassbinder put it, "we were born to need each other, but we haven't learned how to live with each other."

The eleven stories that follow are true, and all except two happened during the period in which I immersed myself in the pickup artist subculture and was given the alias Style, as chronicled in *The Game*. Unlike *The Game*, however, these stories are less about getting the girl and more about the nature of desire itself. They loosely trace the metaphorical arc of a man's dating life, building toward the question that none of the pickup gurus I met while learning the game was able to answer: What do you do after the orgasm?

Fiction writers are lucky: They can hide behind the flawed characters they create. Here, the only flawed character is me. In the process of approaching thousands of people to master the game and myself, the three engines driving my behavior—hereditary instincts, family upbringing, and social forces—came into constant conflict. As a result, I hurt people's feelings, made bad choices, took unhealthy risks, missed important opportunities, and committed irreversible blunders.

I also had some amazing sex.

And therein lies the conflict.

From each of these experiences, I've tried to extract a lesson. And that hasn't been easy. Because some of these experiences never should have happened in the first place.

RULE 1
ATTRACTION
IS NOT A CHOICE

I am sitting on her couch and she is waiting for an answer.

She is offering me French lessons.

She is sitting too close. She is talking too slow. She is accidentally on purpose grazing my knee with the back of her hand.

She wants me.

She has to be at least sixty.

And, somehow, I feel myself drawn in.

I know the symptoms: dizzy, light-headed, eyes defocusing, room melting, PC muscle contracting.

I look at her: she is old, man. And not a good old. Just plain old. And worn-down. Brittle black-gray hair piled sloppily atop her head. Pea-size pores freckling her face. Body like a bag of gravel. Blood-pressure socks. Varicose veins. Granny glasses. Mustache.

I have to get out of here. Before it's too late.

"Gotta get back to writing . . . me, too . . . well, bye then . . . sure, a French lesson would be . . . I'm not sure when . . . work and all . . . but, yeah, definitely . . . and give my best to Josh . . . thanks . . . you, too."

Jesus. That was close.

We have lived on the same floor of the same apartment building in Pasadena for six months. We've passed each other in the hallway many times. She's always with her autistic son, Josh. I feel bad for her. She's a single mother, and has sacrificed her entire life to take care of her son and nurture his autistic musical genius. He knows the name, lyrics, chords, recording date, and catalog number of every Beatles song and is not too shy to recite them to strangers. He never forgets a face or a fact. He has aged her prematurely.

Yet every time I run into her in the hallway or the elevator, there is this tingle. This energy. I feel drawn in and hypnotized. I can't describe it any better. But I know it's attraction. I want to kiss her. It makes no logical sense. The only older women I've slept with were ones any red-blooded boy would go for: long legs, workout bodies, spray tan, shampoo-commercial hair. I've never been drawn to a woman like this before. Yet, sometimes, at night, as I prepare to sleep, my hand will lazily drift into my boxer shorts. And I'll find myself thinking of her.

I live in Los Angeles. I see some of the most gorgeous women in the world on a daily basis. They're everywhere: carrying their crappy little show dogs, sitting in Starbucks on a Tuesday afternoon because they're too pretty to work a day job, jogging along the beach like they're auditioning for *America's Next Top Model*.

And what do I do? I masturbate to the sixty-year-old crone in my building.

I could have anyone in my fantasies. And by this point, I could have just about anyone in real life, too. Why do I keep choosing her?

Two days later, I'm taking the elevator to the garage with the previous night's companion, Darcy. She is sexy but shady. Claims her job is throwing parties for men in Las Vegas. I would like to go to one of those parties sometime.

"Hi, Neil," a loud, nasal voice greets us when we step out of the elevator.

It's Josh. He met Darcy in the building once before, about three weeks ago. He just turned fifteen. He's starting to get acne and feelings around girls he can't explain. He likes to talk to me about masturbation and how he hates his mom.

"Hi, Darcy. You're twenty-six and from Newton in Massachusetts, right?" He knows he's right. Show-off. "You're pretty."

Nancy weak-smiles at us. "I'm sorry. Josh, come on."

I look at Darcy. She is tan from a bottle. She is buxom from a Beverly Hills doctor. She is rail-thin from crystal meth. She is a porcelain doll of youth, sexuality, and doom.

I look at Nancy. She is pasty from indoor lighting. She is saggy from age. She is lumpy from lack of exercise. She has given up on youth, on sexuality, on herself. The autistic cross she's had to bear for so many years has consumed her, broken her, wrecked her.

What was I thinking?

"Hey, Neil, 'The Long and Winding Road' is a good song. Do you like that song?"

"It's great," I tell Josh.

"It was written on the same day as 'Let It Be,' " he informs me. "It's the only song on the album that just has Paul McCartney on piano and not Billy Preston. What do you think he means when he says, 'crying for the day'? What day is he crying for?"

That's the tragedy of Josh. He knows facts. But metaphor is too vague.

"The day when things were better."

"Don't you think he could just mean the day before?"

He is too literal. He doesn't realize that if words only represented their dictionary definitions, they would no longer serve the purpose of expression. There would be no Beatles, no literature, no poetry. There is something underneath each word that affects its expression and interpretation. That thing is called emotion. The inability to recognize it is something both Josh and Darcy have in common.

"Josh, let Neil go," Nancy coos from inside the elevator, finger mashed against the open-door button. Then to me: "He's excited because he's going to stay with his piano teacher tonight."

The door closes. And I wonder what she meant.

Was she just apologizing for his behavior?

Or was she trying to let me know she's going to be alone tonight?

I can't even say for sure that she's ever thought about me in that way. And, surely, after seeing Darcy, she can't expect I'd actually be interested in her.

The whole thing is just ridiculous. I see a lot of potential in Josh, though; I'd like to turn him on to more good music. It would be nice for him to have a mentor closer to his age.

That night, I find myself on Nancy's doorstep. There is a Zombies CD in my hands. I keep telling myself I'm just dropping off a CD for Josh, because I think it'll open up a new world of music for him. But I know why I'm really there: to see what happens.

I don't think I would actually go for it, if given the chance. That would be gross. I just want to satisfy my curiosity. And she seems interesting as a person. Very cultured. I'd like to know about her background: What she was like before she had Josh. How she makes a living. Where she learned French. Stuff like that.

Nancy doesn't seem surprised when she answers the door. She is wearing a black shapeless dress and lumpy stockings, and her cheeks are awkwardly rouged. The sleeves of the dress cinch her arms above her elbow, creating a roll of skin that reminds me of a Polish sausage.

She steps to one side and holds the door open. According to the rules of politeness, I must enter.

Now I am in the lair. And I feel the energy shift around me.

"This is for Josh," I tell her.

She takes the CD from me. Her fingers don't touch mine.

"Would you like some tea?" she offers. "I just made some."

The web is forming.

"Sure."

I sit on the couch. It is burlap, with a yellow-and-white–knit blanket thrown over it. It smells like sandalwood and ashes. I'm having trouble breathing. My chest is tightening. I look at the door. It seems so far away.

I am sunk.

My dick is pushing lightly against the denim of my jeans. What is going on?

I look at Nancy. My grandmother was a prettier lady than her. This doesn't make sense.

She shuffles over with the cup of tea. I thank her.

"*Je vous en prie,*" she responds.

I love it when she speaks French. Her accent is perfect.

We talk about Josh. That is all we ever talk about. He is practicing for a piano recital. He can figure out any song by ear. His teacher is impressed. I can't focus. I can't focus. I can't focus.

She wants to show me pictures. They are in a cream-colored album. She sits next to me, lays it in her lap, and opens it with elegant fingers. The front cover drops onto my left leg.

"This is Josh and his teacher standing outside the Schoenberg Music Building."

I don't see. I don't know. I don't care. My nostrils are filling with her scent. My heart is hammering. The room is spinning. I need to do something to stop it.

I raise my hand and clumsily brush a stray strand of hair off her face. It feels like a pipe cleaner.

She stops speaking, lifts her head, and turns toward me. A blast of sandalwood ash hits me in the face. I must have her.

My lips crush hers. It is like the triumphant last chord of a symphony ringing in my head.

Her lips are rough and bumpy, but her tongue is soft and fat. She just sort of puts it in my mouth. It lays there, and it feels nice. It emits that slow, sensual energy she has, sending it all through my body.

I know this is wrong. I'm fully aware that a line has been crossed.

Fortunately, she senses that I'm uncomfortable.

"Should we go into the bedroom?" she asks.

I am not shocked by this. I actually think that it is a great idea.

She leads the way. I follow, and as I see her body moving in front of me, bulging everywhere with no shape that could be defined as sexual, the spell breaks. For a moment, I have the option to leave. But I don't.

I am compelled by my own nature to finish what I start. And perhaps I never really had the option to leave anyway.

She sits on the edge of what looks like a hospital bed. With effort, she slowly raises her legs off the floor and onto the mattress.

I remove my shoes and join her. She doesn't say anything and neither do I. One word would ruin it.

Her hands wrap around my back. Our tongues reunite. The smell of old lady oozes from her skin. I do not want to take this slowly.

I start to pull off her dress while balancing on top of her, then roll off and let her finish the job.

Her skin is the color of oxidized newspaper. Her underpants end where her bra stops. Both pieces seem excessively large. And they do not match. The underwear is white, the bra is what they call nude. They are about function, not form.

I do not want to linger here. I do not want to linger anywhere.

I reach behind her and release the bra hook by hook. I place a breast in my mouth. It seems like the right thing to do.

I am able to disconnect for a moment, to imagine her as desirable as I circle my tongue around her nipple. Encouraged, I decide to stop looking and retreat into the world of feeling.

But then I reach down to slide off her underwear. And beneath, instead of skin, I feel plastic. I grope around it. There is some sort of plastic bag attached to her side.

I can't remember much after this. I recall a strange wave of nausea coming over me. I recall proceeding anyway because it is my nature. I recall it lasting no more than five minutes. I recall making the minimum amount of necessary conversation afterward to ensure her comfort. And then leaving.

In the days that followed, I didn't think about Nancy much. Not in the way I used to. I talked to her on the phone a couple times afterward, just so she wouldn't think I was avoiding her in the hallway, which I was. I can't say why I no longer fantasized about her. Maybe it was that I'd attributed a certain sensuality to her that didn't exist in reality. Or maybe it was the plastic bag.

A month later, I moved out of the building. Not because of Nancy. Because I felt isolated and listless in Pasadena. I wanted to live where people were struggling and striving and trying to become, because that's always where the action is. That's where you find life. That's where you find beautiful, desperate women, if that's your sort of thing.

I called Nancy and said good-bye. I promised to stay in touch and see Josh's upcoming recital.

That's where the story should end. But it doesn't. In fact, it probably shouldn't have even begun. Nonetheless, seven months later when I was collecting my mail from the building manager, I saw her again.

She looked thin. She'd lost at least thirty pounds. Her hair was clean, dyed black, and tied in a perfect bun atop her head. She was wearing lipstick, mascara, eye shadow. She practically glowed.

On her arm was a man. He appeared to be her age. Small

and bald, but not bad-looking. He was sprightly, well-tanned, confident.

"Hey, you look great," I told her.

"Merci." She seemed happy.

"Where's Josh?"

"I moved him to a different floor," she said in that slow voice that had once charmed me. "He lives in apartment 502 now, with a tutor I found for him."

She fell silent for a moment and smiled thinly at me. She'd even bleached the hair over her lip. *"Merci,"* she repeated.

There was a new energy around Nancy. It wasn't attraction. It was gratitude. I felt like I'd done something nice for her, that I'd unlocked and released something she'd forgotten she had. Perhaps that was the energy I had felt the whole time: an exuberant woman trying to break free from the prison she'd been in since her son was born.

I thought for a moment that maybe I'd found a calling: the angel of fuck. There are, everywhere, women who have given up on their sexuality. I see them in the airport, too scared to break up with the cheating husbands who take them for granted. I see them at the beach, so busy tending to their ungrateful children that they've forgotten to tend to themselves. I see them at the twenty-four-hour diner, still nursing the wounds of a breakup that happened decades ago, watching the twenty-year-old waitresses with hateful eyes, thinking, "Someday. You'll see."

They were all once eighteen and bursting with youth, spirit, sensuality, possibility, and countless potential suitors, one or two or ten or twenty of whom would drain away all that light. I could seduce them. I could slowly, tenderly fuck each and every one of them. I could make them eighteen again. Not for me, but for them. So their sexuality, their passion, their selves could re-awaken, and they'd realize that life still lay ahead of them and eighteen wasn't all that great a year anyway.

I could do that.

As I left the house, climbed into the secondhand SUV I'd just bought, and drove back to my new place in Hollywood, I realized the flaw in my plan: it wasn't me who had seduced and saved Nancy. She had seduced me. And I'd moved. I'd changed. I'd grown up.

Maybe the gratitude I felt was my own.

RULE 2
ONE BROKEN LINK DESTROYS THE CHAIN

Kevin is going to be here any minute. He wants to go out and meet women. And I'm still in my boxer shorts. I have not showered or shaved in days, man. When I look in the mirror, I see the ghost of Yasser Arafat staring back at me.

I should not be going out when I have a book due in fourteen days. But my eyes are going to melt in their sockets if I keep staring at this computer. I've been writing for three weeks straight. It's time to interact with living beings again. My social skills are rusting.

Have to get my act together quickly. My lucky broken vintage Vostok Soviet military watch has somehow time traveled into the kitchen, where it's lying facedown in peanut butter. I need to clean the kitchen. It could be embarrassing if anyone came back here.

I should add that to my list. But first I need to find the list, which is probably in the pocket of my Levi's premium boot-cut jeans. The jeans are in the clothing pile. This is where items go that I've worn but don't smell bad enough to get cleaned yet. It is an altar from which I compose my identity every day.

I had an idea last night for a book that I also need to add to the list. What was it? Something about living without technology for a year.

Shit. There's the buzzer. It's Kevin. Forgot he was coming and he's already here. Get it together, Neil. Kevin needs you to be his sacrificial lamb and start conversations with the beautiful women of Southern California.

Grab Levi's premium boot-cut jeans. Smell jeans. The scent is a cross between macadamia nuts and my room after sex. That'll work.

"Hey." Kevin grins lopsided when I answer the door. "You going out like that?"

Putting on other leg of jeans now. Just have to find a shirt. Something cool. Something from my pile, because if it's cool, I've probably worn it in the last month. And if I've worn it in the last month, I definitely haven't washed it.

Fish for black shirt. When in doubt, wear black. It's the safety net of male fashion. Grab tail of gray knit tie I bought in London and pull loose from pile. The tie looks puffy. I may have accidentally washed it last month.

Just need a belt. Must sort through pile to find belt. Every item tells a story. This yellowy T-shirt I picked up seven years ago at a Boston warehouse that sells clothing for a dollar a pound.

"Hey, man, it's gonna be crowded if we don't get there soon," Kevin says. He shows up late and he's mad at me, like I'm some kind of dawdler.

Just use puffy gray tie as belt. Now need something around

neck. Pendant necklace? Too disco. Shoelace? Too thin. Red ribbon from Christmas present? Fine. It's like nature's own silk tie.

"Ready?"

"Ready."

"Like that?"

"I'll be fine. I can rely on my charm."

Kevin is my friend, but not really. If my car broke down, he's not someone I would call to fetch me. We are united only by our shared pursuit of women.

"Remember the girl I had call you the other night?" he asks as I unlock my car door. Somewhere underneath these Coke bottles and Red Bull cans, there is a driver's seat. "I brought her home and we were gonna get in the Jacuzzi, but my mom fucking drained it." There's precious, life-giving Red Bull left in this can. Need my taurine. "So we got in anyway, and she gave me head while I looked at the stars." Kevin is sitting on my rough draft.

Feel like there's fog in my head. Gotta clear it out. Get present in the moment. Clap my hands. Shake my head. Use my voice box.

"Testing, testing." It works.

"What are you doing?" Kevin asks.

"Warming up."

Drive 2.3 miles to James Beach bar, hand valet keys, smile, enter, pretend to be normal. Girls everywhere, drinking, laughing, each one unique and growing ever more intoxicated by the sudden smell of macadamia nuts in the room.

Two women who appear to be in their twenties walk away from the bar. Must start talking or I'll be stuck in my head all night. I feel Kevin's hand on my back pushing me toward them. I should package Kevin's hand and sell it to men who are too scared to approach women.

"Have you met my friend Kevin?" I ask. "He's in the world's only all-Jewish Christian rock band."

"A what?" asks one of the girls. Model tall, stringy blonde hair, sand-dollar complexion, white jacket with rainbow buttons. Seems like the kind of girl you'd meet at one of those bookstores that sell incense at the cash register.

"He's in a band," I repeat.

"So am I," she says. She is friendly and kind of sweet. I didn't expect her to take me seriously. I suppose rainbow buttons are a sign of tolerance.

Her friend has a tight white tube top, compact frame, long black hair, angular face. The kind of girl you'd meet in the sales office of a gym.

I need to start going to the gym again. And eating healthier. And flossing every night. I'm losing it all.

"Is that peanut butter on your watch?" Bookgirl asks, touching my hand.

"Don't manhandle it. It's vintage Soviet military peanut butter. Worth a fortune."

As Kevin and I talk to Bookgirl and Gymgirl, we automatically pair off. Why do I bother to write? This is so much more fun.

"You have one life to live." I hear myself telling Bookgirl. The words are not mine. They belong to Joseph Campbell, dead professor of mythology. "Marx teaches us to blame society for our frailties, Freud teaches us to blame our parents, and astrology teaches us to blame the universe." The fog has lifted. It's funny how quickly it comes back. I constantly forget that people tend to be polite, unless they think you want something from them, which, of course, we do. "But the only place to look for blame is if you didn't have the guts to bring out your full self, if you didn't act on your desires, if you didn't take advantage of what was in front of you and live the life that was your potential."

There are tears in her eyes. Thank you, Joseph Campbell. I take her hand in mine and she squeezes it warmly. Forgot to clip my nails. Have to add that to the list. I keep a list in my head of things I need to add to the list in my pocket.

"That's just what I needed to hear," she says, and takes another sip of beer, "because I'm three months pregnant, and I'm just asking a lot of questions right now."

For some reason, I am not fazed by this. I look at Gymgirl. Kevin is massaging her shoulders and whispering in her ear. I make out the words "anal sex."

Bookgirl tells me she lives with her boyfriend and loves him very much. She tells me her friend is married and has two children and loves them very much.

The night is dark.

I was introduced to Prince once in a bar, and he asked me what I did. I told him I wrote books. He asked what they were about, and I said they were about the dark side. "Why the dark side?" he asked.

"Because it's more interesting," I told him.

"But the light side can be interesting, too," he admonished.

I wish Prince were here right now. He would see that he was wrong. Every adventure to be had in this room is on the dark side. The people on the light side are asleep right now. And they are dreaming about the dark side. Because the more you try to repress the dark side, the stronger it gets, until it finds its own way to the surface. I sleep well. I dream of angels and sponge cakes and panda bears. I don't see the dark side until I open my eyes. And, tonight, it seems the dark side is going to be a pregnant New Age Amazonian who lives with her loving boyfriend.

"Will you take us to our car?" Gymgirl asks when the bar closes. "We don't like walking alone late at night."

"That will cost extra," Kevin tells them. They don't laugh. "Just wait a sec while we find our friends."

Of course, we have no friends here. This is Kevin's way of getting me alone to make a plan. And that is great. Because I enjoy plans.

"Okay," I conspire with him. "Let's tell them that our friends left without us, and we need a ride home."

"Love it. What about your car?"

"We'll just leave it with the valet and pick it up tomorrow."

The girls agree to take us home without hesitation. A simple plan can make all the difference between going home with company and going home alone.

We're walking down the street now, arm in arm. We are saving them from criminals. They are saving us from taxicab drivers. It's a fair trade.

"Wow, it's funny how we paired off into couples," Bookgirl says. My head reaches her shoulders. And if she doesn't care, I don't care.

Their car is a BMW convertible, which indicates that they surely could have afforded the valet. Maybe they also had a plan.

Bookgirl wants to play me her music. This concerns me, but it also allows me to proceed with stage two of our plan.

"This sounds great," I tell her. It is sappy and makes me want to punch butterflies. "But it's too windy to hear your lyrics. Just bring it upstairs and we can play it where it's more quiet."

She agrees.

Women are not stupid: She knows what she's just agreed to. We park and walk arm-in-arm to my front door. Infidelity is in the air. It is dark and smells like macadamia nuts.

I reach into my pocket to grab the keys.

They are not there.

I double-check my pockets, as if everything's just fine. Give myself a full-body pat down. I feel the potential of the evening begin to dissipate.

The girls are looking at me suspiciously now. All the doubts that liquor and smooth talk held back are creeping to the surface of their minds with each passing second. They know something is up.

Okay. No need to panic. Obviously, I must have my keys because I drove to the club. Otherwise . . .

Fuck. I'm an idiot. I valeted the car. So the valet still has my keys. And I'm locked out.

In the blink of an eye, I develop a plan. There's always a plan.

"I left my keys upstairs," I tell the girls. "But it's no problem. I'm just going to climb up to the balcony. I always do this."

I never do this.

"What floor do you live on?" Gymgirl asks. Good question.

"The third. Just wait right there. I'll be back in a second."

I run to the side of the building and look up. This is possible. It's just a puzzle. And every puzzle has a solution.

Gotta think quickly. I'm losing them.

I believe I can make it. No problem. If I fall, I die.

The girls follow me and look up the side of the building doubtfully. "I'm getting kind of tired," Bookgirl says. "I should probably go home."

I suppose this makes sense. After all, she is pregnant. And I really should not be having sex with her.

"This'll only take a second," I tell her. "Just wait at the front door, and I'll be right there to let you in. Don't worry about it."

It is time to save the night.

I climb onto the first-floor railing. It's loose and shakes beneath my feet. I did not plan on this. Have to move fast.

Grab the bottom of the second-floor balcony and pull myself up. Forearms shaking. Shouldn't have stopped going to the gym. Kick my legs over. A little winded. Take a short break here with the rear of my Levi's premium boot-cut jeans hanging in the air.

Okay, just have to pull my upper body up now. Quietly. If I wake anyone, they may call the police. Or shoot me.

On the second floor now. Everything is under control. Just repeat, and I'll be on my balcony and home, having sex with this girl and her embryo.

I stretch and grab the base of my balcony railing, then hoist myself up and kick my legs onto the ledge. I am almost home. Just need to pull my body up so my jeans aren't hanging in the air.

There is a slight problem. I can't move. My tie-belt is caught on something. Can't see it from this position. Probably a nail.

Must use brute force. I pull hard on the balcony railing. Forearms getting tired. Now the railing is bending toward me. This is not good.

They really make strong ties in London.

Think, Neil. Think. You're smarter than this nail.

There is a hotel across the street. Maybe I can signal to someone in the window. But what would they do? Probably just call the fire department and make a big scene.

Need to retrace my steps. Unclimb the building.

I lower myself back to the second floor and the tie slips off a rusty nail that probably once held a planter.

Standing on the second-floor balcony, I remove the tie-belt and stuff it in my pocket. The jeans slip halfway down my ass. Won't be able to climb with pants falling off. Need to remove them.

I take off my boots, step out of my Levi's premium boot-cut jeans, lean over the edge of the railing, and toss them up to my balcony.

They plummet to the pavement below.

When I look down to see if the jeans survived, I notice headlights in the street. It's a convertible. The girls are leaving. The night is ruined. I knew I should have stayed in and written. Why do I let Kevin talk me into these things?

"It's okay," Kevin yells, as I'm putting my boots back on. "The married girl is coming back."

He is talking way too loud. He's going to wake the whole neighborhood.

"I think we can double-team her," he shouts.

"Shh," I admonish him.

A light inside the apartment I'm standing outside flips on. And I'm on their balcony in boxer shorts and one boot.

There is only one way to save the situation. I race to the railing, climb on top of it, then spring onto my balcony. It all happens so fast, and in such a panic, that I don't even know how I did it. I may have just proven the theory of evolution. Surely, if I can access the climbing genes of my ancient monkey ancestors, I can live without technology for that book idea.

What a horrible night. And my room is a mess. Clothes are everywhere. My heart is hammering. Gotta remember to get my boot off the downstairs balcony later.

And pick up my jeans from the street.

And retrieve my keys and car from 2.3 miles away.

Have to add all this to my list. But first I absolutely must check my e-mail. Something important could have arrived that I may need to deal with. The glow of the computer screen and grinding of the hard drive soothes my nerves. This is where I belong. It's a jungle out there.

Kristen is coming to town and wants to stay with me. Magnus wants me to meet some Norwegian rappers. And Stephen Lynch wants me to send clips of an article I wrote about him.

I have a book due in two weeks. I can't possibly do any of these things. So I write and tell Kristen I'm working on a book, but she can stay as long as she understands that I need to write. I tell Magnus that I'm working on a book, but I can meet them really quickly for dinner, since I need to eat anyway. And I tell Stephen Lynch that I'm too busy to send his clips right now.

Clip my nails. Must add that to my list right now before I forget again.

The buzzer. Who could that be at this hour?

"What the fuck are you doing up there?"

"I'll be right down."

Kevin is sitting in front of my building. He is not happy with me. I'm probably not the kind of friend he'd call if his car broke down.

"Take that ribbon off your neck," he snaps. "You look ridiculous."

We wait and wait and wait. Gymgirl returns, then tells us she's tired and wants to go home. And I'm okay with that. After all, she is married. And we really should not be having group sex with her.

Sometimes mistakes happen for a reason. I need to write my book anyway. It's due in fourteen days. Actually, thirteen days now.

And a book is a lot of work. It requires a massive amount of organization and planning. Fortunately, these are things I'm good at.

RULE 3
GAME IS A
BORDERLESS STATE

I am writing this in case anything bad happens.

If I disappear, please come looking for me.

Just remember the name Ali Raj. He's a magician, but he may have an illegal sideline. He's supposedly friends with the prime minister's son. And on the off chance that I'm breaking some taboo here, I want you to know what happened.

I love the game. And I believe I may be an addict. It's changed my life in ways I never thought possible. In high school and college, my friends came back from winter and spring breaks talking about their vacation hookups. I never got anything on vacation but a sunburn and a refrigerator magnet. I was never able to just relax and have fun. I was too busy worrying about what everyone else thought of me.

But once I learned the game, everything changed. Wherever I went, new adventures beckoned. I visited Croatia and ended up having sex in the ocean with a nineteen-year-old who hardly spoke a word of English. I flew to a small town in the Midwest for a *New*

York Times article and fooled around with a rich housewife, then slept with her niece. And on my first night in Sweden, I met a girl who stripteased to ABBA in my hotel room as foreplay.

Now I'm in Bangladesh, where there are no clubs, no alcohol, and no dating. And I have options.

But I don't know the rules here. And I'm worried that I'm about to get myself killed.

I'm staying at the Dhaka Sheraton. The only other person who knows me here is my traveling companion, Franz Harary, the illusionist. He has longish blond hair, usually wears yellow shirts with puffy patches on the chest, and has a very gentle demeanor. Think Yanni with magic tricks.

He thinks I'm sick right now.

But I'm in my hotel room, waiting for Tripti to arrive, hoping that Ali Raj and his henchman don't get here first.

Here, really quickly, is how this all started:

Harary is here at the invitation of Ali Raj to perform at the First International Magic Festival. I'm here working on a book that I haven't told anyone about. I've been traveling the world in search of people with powers that defy scientific explanation. I want to find real magic, proof of the existence of the unknown, something to believe in. And there's a village on the outskirts of Dhaka, the capital city here, populated by a small tribe with a blind elder who can supposedly perform miracles on command.

Both the festival and the village are frowned on by local authorities. Bangladesh is largely a Muslim society and, as such, considers magic and miracle working a sin. According to strict Islamic law, these acts are punishable by death. Importing magicians from all over the world is a luxury that only a man like Ali Raj, with a lot of money and high-level government connections, could have made possible.

We first saw Ali Raj himself when we cleared customs. Lean, with perfectly feathered black hair and a dark walking suit, he reminded me of a wax statue of a matador. I don't believe he ever spoke a word. Trailed by a motley entourage of magicians, goons, relatives, and cologne-splattered men who identified themselves as traders, he led us to a press conference that had been set up in an airport waiting room.

The reporters clustered around Harary, who made a Coke bottle—the symbol of America—vanish for the cameras. The reporters were amazed, but Ali Raj was not. He nodded to one of his henchmen, a fat-faced Bangladeshi with a fanny pack, who ended the press conference.

Raj's men herded Harary and me into a minivan with the magicians. As we drove through the crowded streets of Dhaka, women with missing teeth and bleeding gums, men with fist-size tumors on their faces, and children with club feet and shredded lungi skirts swarmed the van at every red light, begging for change. And though the poverty was appalling, the people in the street seemed happier than the average middle-class American. I suppose if you've never had anything, you don't have anything to lose—just surviving is an accomplishment. At home, we tend to take unlimited upward mobility for granted.

I saw Tripti for the first time in the hotel lobby as I was returning to my room from breakfast the next morning. She stood out not just because she was the only female in sight, but because she was wrapped in an immaculate all-white sari with a matching sequined shawl around her neck. She had long black hair, the full lips of a supermodel, and large, round breasts that seemed to lift the fabric away from her body.

She was standing with Ali Raj, so I assumed she must be his wife and I shouldn't be staring at her breasts.

Raj, as usual, didn't speak. "Harary?" she asked through perfectly formed lips.

"He's up in his room working on the helicopter vanish," I told her. Raj translated, and we entered the elevator together.

"I like," she said, touching my earrings.

The earrings are silver spikes I bought after learning about a concept called peacocking. The idea is that, just as the peacock spreads its colorful plumage in order to attract the female of the species, so, too, must a man stand out in order to attract the opposite sex. Though I was initially skeptical, once I began experimenting with these items, as obnoxious and uncool as they seemed, the results were immediate—even in Bangladesh.

She gestured to my shaved head and asked, "I touch?" Without waiting for an answer, she rubbed her hand warmly on my head. Women in Bangladesh rarely get this physical in public with men. Her touching my ears and head was the equivalent of a woman grabbing your crotch in an elevator in America.

I led them to Harary's room and took my leave as he gave Ali Raj his requirements for the illusion—a helicopter, a pilot, a field, and a helicopter-size sheet.

For the rest of the day, Tripti sat at a table in the hotel lobby, selling tickets to the magic show with the rest of Ali Raj's team.

Every time I walked past, she shot me a lingering glance that conveyed an invitation to so much pleasure.

So I decided to accept the invitation.

"Why don't you take a break and get some lunch with me?" I suggested.

She looked at me sweetly and smiled blankly.

Translation: Keep it simple.

"Lunch?"

As she tried to explain something too complicated for broken English, a short, muscular Bangladeshi man with black hair and a red shirt arrived with two Styrofoam dishes of some rice concoction he'd bought in the street.

I introduced myself. "I am Rashid, my friend," he replied. "I am cousin to Tripti."

"Do you also work for Ali Raj?"

He nodded in the affirmative. Everyone works for Ali Raj.

I suggested that we all eat together upstairs. If I couldn't get her alone, at least I could win the trust of her cousin. This was Bangladesh; I wasn't expecting to get very far anyway.

I took them to Harary's room and sat with them on the couch. Tripti's cousin politely handed me one of the rice dishes. I tried a small spoonful, and some sort of hot, deadly venom seared my internal organs.

"You like, my friend?" he asked. It's interesting how whenever someone calls you his friend when you're not really his friend, it sounds malicious.

"It's great," I choked.

Sometimes, in the heat of passion, there's a temptation to have sex without a condom. At that moment, I felt like I had performed the culinary equivalent: every guidebook warned against eating street food in Bangladesh.

Between the sexual energy emanating from Tripti, the brutal spiciness of the rice dish, and the awkwardness of the situation, beads of sweat began sprouting on my forehead. It was ridiculous to think I could have an affair with this girl. Our cultures are too different when it comes to dating and sex. We prefer premarital sex; they prefer arranged marriages.

I decided to cut my losses and take a nap in my room. This just wasn't worth risking days of diarrhea.

As I rose to leave, however, Tripti turned and whispered something in her cousin's ear. He nodded, then she stood up to join me.

When I walked into the hallway, she followed. So I led her to my room, uncertain of what she wanted or expected.

As we entered, I was mindful to leave the door open so she didn't feel uncomfortable. I wanted to demonstrate that I understood the morals of her society.

I sat down on the bed and she maneuvered into position next to me, too close for conversation. Suddenly, diarrhea seemed like a worthwhile risk.

I've seen many Bollywood movies, and one of the strangest things about them is that the hero and heroine never actually kiss. Instead, they just come excruciatingly close to doing so all through the film. So I stroked Tripti's hair. She didn't flinch. I looked her in the eyes and brought my lips close. She smelled like muscat, like desire, like something forbidden.

Suddenly, she pulled away. Then she stood up and walked toward the door. Perhaps I'd been too forward and misinterpreted her actions.

Instead of leaving, however, she closed the door. "I like you," she said as she walked back toward the bed.

Evidently she was more a fan of Hollywood films than Bollywood—which are Indian anyway. So I threw her onto the bed and we began making out.

This was where things began to get weird. I realize they were already weird, but they got weirder.

She placed my hands on her breasts and began speaking in a stream of fractured Bengali-English. It came breathy, in my ear, difficult to make out. All I could catch were the names "Bill Clinton" and "Monica Lewinsky."

And this completely confused me, because I wasn't sure if she was offering me a blow job using the only English words she knew as a synonym, or if she was simply sharing her thoughts on American politics.

Assuming the best, I decided to try to remove her sari. Never having actually removed a sari before, I wasn't sure where to start.

She shivered with pleasure as I fumbled around her neckline, then she yanked my hand away. "I good girl," she said. "It is okay. I like you."

Translation: "I don't normally do this, but actually I do normally do this. I just don't want you to think I normally do this."

She unbuttoned my shirt and ran her fingers along my chest. Her other arm leaned directly against the bulge in my pants. Then she began whispering, over and over, sensually. At first I thought she was saying "*cholo*." But the tenth time around, I sounded it out as "*chulatay*."

Every cell in my body was vibrating with desire for her, while every cell in my brain tried to compute how and why this was happening.

Three *chulatays* later, she disentangled herself, straightened her sari, and stood up as if nothing had just happened. "No person," she said as she put a finger to her lips.

Translation: Either "Don't tell anybody" or "I will kiss no one else because we're now engaged."

Then she said the two words that struck fear in my heart, "Ali Raj," and made a slashing motion over her neck.

"Good girl," she repeated.

I knew I was in over my head. Yet something inside propelled me to proceed. Perhaps it was the same impulse that compels a child, when someone draws an imaginary line in the grass with the toe of his shoe and orders him not to cross it "or else," to gingerly dip his foot on the forbidden side of the line in response. It's not just an act of defiance, it's a call for adventure. His side of the line is boring; the other side contains the unknown, the "or else." The Ali Raj.

While waiting for the festival to begin that night, I made it my mission to find out what *chulatay* meant. I eventually narrowed it down to one of two interpretations: either "hanging" or "I'm hungry." Hopefully, the latter interpretation was correct.

That night, the streets around the magic show swarmed with police and reporters. The theater was in a university neighborhood, the center of Islamic radicalism, and there had been several bomb threats. Every time someone bicycled past with a package in his handbasket, I imagined the next day's headline: "Terrorists Make Magicians Disappear." Nonetheless, I headed inside. Who wants to live in a world without magic?

I found Tripti walking through the foyer and led her to the back row. As an illusionist from Spain named Juan Mayoral performed some sort of magical love soliloquy to a wire mannequin, Tripti took hold of my inner thigh. She squeezed it and, her breath wet in my ear, whispered, "How is Babu?" She then began rubbing Babu through my pants.

I looked around the theater: there were Bangladeshi men everywhere and a few scattered families. Everyone was staid, mannered, reserved, intent on the show, and I had this Muslim girl moaning in my ear. Every man has his secret fantasy: This, I realized, was mine.

As happens with most fantasies, however, reality soon intruded. The fanny pack-wearing Ali Raj henchman from the press conference plopped down in the seat next to me. Tripti quickly withdrew her hand.

"Are you married?" he asked. He knew exactly what was going on.

"No," I told him.

"Will you marry her?"

"I just met her." I couldn't tell if he was cockblocking, or if this was all some kind of plan to marry Tripti off to an American.

Between acts, I decided to try to find a secluded place to take Tripti. There were all kinds of stairwells and rooms backstage. But when we stood up, Fanny Pack rose with us and cleaved closely to our sides.

"My friend," a voice greeted me as I walked into the foyer with my growing entourage. It was her cousin. My enemy. All men here were my enemies.

He threw his right arm around my shoulder. "This is the American writer," he said to three nearby men, who were either family or Ali Raj henchmen or both. They circled me and all began friending me at once. Whenever I craned my head to look for Tripti, they redirected my attention to their conversation: "Is this your first time in Bangladesh?" "How do you like Bangladesh?" "You must come to my home for traditional Bengali dinner."

Finally, I caught sight of Tripti, who seemed either oblivious to her protective barrier or pretending to be in order to preserve her honor. I whisked her into the theater, but the phalanx of Bangladeshi men followed, tripping to get ahead of us, between us, alongside us.

When we sat down, they arranged themselves everywhere around us. Fanny Pack motioned for Tripti to move over, took her seat, and spread his legs until his knees touched mine. It all felt malevolent. As if, instead of fighting, they just got real friendly here.

"So you like Tripti? Maybe you meet her mother and father?"

Just then, I felt a sharp kick in my abdomen. I doubled over with pain.

The spicy rice had done its damage.

That night, I returned to the hotel in defeat. I spent the next hour on the toilet letting go of my need to get laid in Bangladesh. In the morning, I popped an Imodium so I could visit the miracle village with Harary later that day.

In the lobby, I saw Tripti in her usual spot at the ticket table, looking radiant in a heavily beaded all-black sari.

"Ali Raj say no leave table," she said fearfully.

I was dumbfounded by the degree of effort these men were making to keep us apart. It was as if we'd been swept up in some epic romance: two lovers from different cultures separated by family—and an evil magician.

These obstacles only served to intensify my desire for her. So, like a fish compelled by hunger toward the worm of its own doom, I made a desperate move and did one of the most clichéd things I can lay claim to in a long tradition of clichéd behavior in pursuit of women: I handed her the key card for my hotel room.

"Tonight, no magic," I told her. "Come here. I wait."

"But Ali Raj," she protested. I was sick of hearing those two words.

"No Ali Raj," I said. "You. Me. Tonight. Last chance."

I sounded less like I was seducing her and more like I was having a going-out-of-business sale.

After a moment of reflection, she responded slowly, gravely, "Okay, I come."

To give her a plausible excuse to visit me, I purposely left my sunglasses lying on the ticket table. It seemed romantic in a sleazy sort of way.

Then I walked out of the hotel to join Harary in the van scheduled to take us to the miracle village. The only problem was that the trip had been arranged by Ali Raj. Everything was arranged by Ali Raj. So the van was full of my new friends. The only one I felt I could trust was a sweet older magician wearing a polyester suit two sizes too large for him. His name was Iqbal.

Fanny Pack took a seat next to me, threw his bullying arm around me, and asked, with a slow smile and wink, "You sleep well, my friend?"

"Fine," I muttered. I wanted to get away from him. This friend shit was clearly the Bengali equivalent of Chinese water torture.

"What is this?" Fanny Pack asked, reaching across with his other arm to touch the zipper on my jeans.

"Dude, what is your problem?" I leapt up and took a seat next to Iqbal. Cockblocking I understood, but cocktouching was completely new to me.

"If we were in America, I'd smash his face in," I told Iqbal. Their head games were clearly getting to me.

"The men here like to control the women," he said patiently. "There are more acid attacks in Bangladesh than any other country."

Acid attacks?

"Yes, when men throw acid in the faces of women who reject them. It is better now because of strict laws."

Bangladesh had successfully beat me. Scared me away from its women. It wasn't worth risking Tripti's disfigurement just so I could have a local girlfriend I'd never see again. I was in no shape for sex anyway: My stomach felt like it was trying to digest a sea urchin shell. I needed to find her when we returned and call off tonight's escapade.

After another hour and a half of bumpy, bowel-jiggling roads, we arrived at the village, a collection of crudely painted shacks in a barren field of dirt. No one had digital satellite TV or a subscription to *InStyle*, so we were the entertainment—especially since

Harary had brought a film crew to capture him fraternizing with the locals.

The women were beautifully made up and covered head to toe in jewelry. As we walked around, I noticed a group of teenage girls following me and staring. Eventually, a few worked up the courage to approach and began gesturing to my earrings, bracelets, rings, and shaved head.

I asked Iqbal to talk to the women and find out what they were up to. "All the women, they like you," he came back and told me. Then he pointed out a pair of barefoot, bejeweled beauty queens and said, "Those girls want to marry you."

"Why don't they want to marry Harary? He's the one all the cameras are following."

Iqbal talked to them a moment, then turned and smiled. "They like you."

In that moment, I learned that the game is universal. Peacocking—the rule of standing out rather than fitting in, of embodying a more exciting lifestyle instead of the one people are used to—seems to work in every culture. I was now officially doomed to dress ridiculously for the rest of my single life.

When we met the miracle-working village elder, I discovered something else that was universal: the principles of magic. Her miracles were just sleight-of-hand tricks, originally and masterfully executed using chicken bones. We then watched a snake charmer antagonizing a snake that had been devenomed, and a man performing an old fakir trick in which he swallowed a string and then appeared to pull it out of his stomach.

So what we discovered was not people with powers we couldn't explain, but a village of magicians who've passed down tricks from generation to generation—and who travel door to door in other villages, performing these tricks for money. In other words, we found a village full of beggar Franz Hararys.

When we returned to the hotel, the ticket table was abandoned and Tripti was gone. I had no way to get in touch with her and cancel our illicit rendezvous.

So here I am, at 8:25 p.m. in Dhaka, sitting in my hotel room, waiting for Tripti to arrive, killing time by crapping out my intestines and researching acid attacks on Google. There are as many as 341 attacks in Bangladesh a year, most of which involve women. The weapon of choice is sulfuric acid, usually poured from a car battery into a cup and then thrown on the woman's face. The disfigurement that results is more hideous than anything I've seen in a horror film. And these women are the lucky ones. The unlucky ones are forced to drink the acid.

Of course, I could be horribly wrong about Ali Raj and his men. Perhaps they're actually on my side and protecting me from Tripti. Maybe they want to save me from a marriage trap she is laying.

Or maybe they're not actually cockblocking but hitting on me. According to one Web site, five percent of Bangladesh's population is homosexual.

I wish she'd get here already. The Internet is a dangerous tool in the hands of a paranoid man with time to kill.

Five Google searches later, I hear footsteps in the hall. Getting closer. A knock. Why doesn't she just use the key I gave her?

I hear her voice. There's a man's voice, too. She's with someone. This is not a good sign.

"Be right there!"

I'm going to e-mail this to myself. Hopefully, someone will check my account and find it if anything happens to me. Maybe I should copy Bernard just in case.

Wish me luck. Or don't. I probably deserve whatever's coming to me.

... AND THEN ...

RULE 4
KNOW THE TERRAIN
BEFORE TAKING THE JOURNEY

MAGGIE

Maggie climbed, dripping, out of the backyard swimming pool, perfumed in gardenia and chlorine. The water pooled in small bulbs on the ridges of bone in her neck, the shelves of young muscle in her abdomen, the disappearing baby fat of her thighs.

She strode toward me, as fast as happiness, and I led her upstairs, my steps heavy on the white plush carpet. I was envious of the way she existed so completely and freely in each moment, and fought to clear the maelstrom of anxieties that circled my mind like wolves hunting a deer.

I flipped her onto the bed and, as she hit the mattress, a giggle dislodged, filling my bare white room with the sound of female. She lay there and waited for what she knew would come next. If I could just press my body tightly enough against hers, thrust myself deeply enough into her, slow my heartbeat enough to match hers, then I, too, could feel young and free and happy.

I'm not sure what she wanted from me, a man twelve years

older, out of shape, and consumed by worry over another deadline in an endless series of deadlines. Perhaps she wanted acceptance, unaware that the need for it is not only insatiable but the cause of most mistakes made in life. Perhaps she wanted maturity, un- aware that it's just a cage adults make children race toward so that they may one day be as miserable as them. Or perhaps she was so carefree that she didn't want anything except to give.

LINDA

Linda wiped away a snail track of sweat running down her temple, biting her lower lip for my benefit. She straddled me cautiously, her legs and arms tense against the bed to prevent full surrender. Her body was long and agile, like a ballerina's but with a woman's hips, and thick brown hair flowed over her flat curves, hiding a nakedness that still felt dirty to her. Her lips were swollen with kisses, her cheeks flushed with the hours of passion it took to get her to this point. Every particle of air in the sparse bedroom—the one she'd grown up in, cleared of childish reminders of who she'd been—was filled with her energy, her intensity, her nervous ex- citement. This was it.

"Go slow," she said. "Be gentle," she said. "Only maybe for a second," she said. Everything a girl would say after making the decision to have sex for the first time, she said.

And then she hesitated, like an orange bobbing on the branch one last time before breaking off its stem. Over the years, she had imagined this act in so many variations of scenery and colors of emotion, denying suitor after suitor who wanted to take it from her because they were like bounty hunters who wanted to put an outlaw in jail not to serve justice, but so they could claim the reward. It had to be just right, so that ten or twenty or thirty years later, she could call to mind every sensation and smile with the conviction that she'd done the right thing.

A giggle—nervous, childlike, womanly, awkward—escaped from her lips as she lifted herself and turned around decisively, sitting astride my bony hips and facing my feet. She set her gaze on a rectangular mirror atop the flimsy pine dresser that had loyally kept her secrets through every age, stage, and metamorphosis. She watched closely as she twisted her torso a little to the left, so that it arced like a model's, then focused her gaze on her face, so she could see what it would look like in the moment of surrender that she so carefully controlled. This was not about me; it was about her. And, in a slow second, charged with nineteen years of being a daughter and a sister and a child, it was done.

ME

And now I sit with them, Maggie on the left in summer dress, Linda on the right in suede skirt, both holding my hand, both thinking I will take them home tonight.

Their grips mirror their beliefs: Maggie's hand lies softly over mine, without worry or urgency, because she knows there will be plenty of time for intimacy later. But she is wrong. She is unaware that two feet away, the hand of her younger sister squeezes mine tightly, possessively, in tacit conspiracy. In her innocence, Maggie has allowed her conniving sister to accompany her on this date. And so the plot in the theater seats is thicker than that on the screen. Two sisters torn apart by a worthless man. And just like

Esau and Jacob, Aaron and Moses, Bart and Lisa, the younger must win. That is the way of things.

And I, who thought I was the great seducer, who boasted of sleeping with model sisters, who validated himself in their embrace like a vampire drinking youth, was nothing more than a doll in their playset.

"We connected right away on a very deep level," Linda had told me that first night in bed. "But then Maggie threw herself at you, so I was just like, whatever."

But perhaps we'd never connected until Maggie claimed me. Perhaps, like me, Linda envied Maggie's freedom and spontaneity, and wanted to take away something of her older sister's. Perhaps she'd decided, on a subconscious level, to lose her virginity with the worst of intentions. And then, with love in her heart, with a smile on her face, with innocence in her eyes, she could once more make her sister feel like the black sheep. Perhaps waiting so long to lose her virginity was never a moral choice for herself, but one intended to make her sister seem like a slut in comparison.

The weapon of the youngest is never physical strength but emotional cunning. And now I am complicit in this trap. I must play my role: Maggie has slept with twenty-six men; I am just a footnote in her sexual history. But I am Linda's entire sexual history and its caretaker. I must keep her memory of the moment preserved in a bell glass. If it shatters, and one shard punctures her heart, the damage will be permanent. She is too smart: She chose the right man, one cursed with a conscience, which dictates that I not ruin her—or any woman—for other men.

And so I have no choice. Someone is going to get hurt tonight, and better the happy slut than the melancholy prude.

Maggie will never forgive me for this, nor will she ever forgive Linda. As I lie in her younger sister's bed that night, Maggie consoles herself with an ex-boyfriend.

A month later, with love in her heart, a smile on her face, and innocence in her eyes, Linda tells me—the one-man army she has used to stage her coup—that Maggie has moved in with him. Three months later, he has gotten Maggie hooked on crystal meth. A year later, Maggie has broken up with him for abusing her. Two and a half years later, Maggie is no longer recognizable as the carefree youth who once climbed dripping out of my swimming pool. She has married him. And, like air bubbles trapped in cement, the decisions we make in a moment haunt us for the rest of our lives.

RULE 5
WHAT YOU PERCEIVE
IS WHO YOU ARE

She said she would pick me up in an old car.

"You'll hear it before you see it." Apologetically.

It was the first time I'd fallen in love with a car.

It was from 1972 and looked worse for the wear. The surface was pocked with small dents, dings, and patches of primer; the bumpers were rusty and looked like they'd seen a lot of action in their day; and the leather interior was torn up from years of constant use and neglect.

But its body was beautiful. It was sinuous and curvy, without a single flat edge; its front tire wells arched smoothly above the surface on either side, sloping into a hood so long you couldn't see the end of it from the passenger seat. When it glided out of the Phoenix airport, people turned their heads. It stood out from the other cars. It was magnificent, proud, unafraid of its defects because it knew its body shape compensated.

"This was the last year they made Corvettes like this," she said. "After 1972, they switched to plastic bumpers."

Her name was Leslie. And, though I'd never met her before, I was going to sleep with her. It was prearranged. Justin, one of my students, had offered me his cousin as a birthday present. It was above and beyond the call of duty. Normally I wouldn't have taken him up on such a creepy proposal, but he promised me that she wasn't just a lay. She was an education.

"She's been studying Tantric sexuality half her life," he said. "And she's discovered a G-spot in the back of her throat."

"That's kind of interesting," I replied, meaning weird. "How does that work exactly? Am I supposed to stick my finger down her throat and massage it?"

"No, something else." He smiled. "She's like a deep throat expert. She can take it all the way in, and work her throat muscles to make you experience something you've never felt before. This is next-level shit."

I was interested, in the classic sense of the word.

A newspaper columnist named Fanny Fern coined the expression that the way to a man's heart is through his stomach, proving to the world just how little women know about men. We can always go out to eat. But if a woman wants to make an impression that we'll never forget, even when we're eighty and on our deathbed and thinking about the two moments that made life worth living, all she has to do is give us the most masterful blow job of our lives. If she even hints that she's great at it, we'll chase her all night. Then, if she actually delivers, she'll never have to worry about a phone call the next day.

It's funny how much time women spend trying to figure us out when we're so simple. I think what's complicated is accepting how simple we actually are.

As Justin pitched me on his cousin, I thought about all the people in my lifetime who had promised to get me laid and never delivered. I remembered Marilyn Manson's bodyguard telling me he had two girls in his hotel room giving a sex show, but because he was married and couldn't sleep with them, he'd send them to me. I lay expectant in my hotel bed for hours, fresh from the shower, trying to stay awake in case sleep turned my breath bad, waiting for the knock. But the knock never came.

Only I came. Alone. Again.

So before my next trip to Phoenix, just to be safe, I called a thin, buxom Iranian girl named Farah, with heavy-lidded, glittering brown eyes. I'd met her last time I was in Phoenix and she mentioned buying a book on Tantric sex. This way, I figured, the Tantra thing would happen one way or the other.

"Yeah, I'm living with my father for now in Sedona," Leslie gabbed as we drove to the James Hotel. "I stay with my sponsor sometimes in Scottsdale, but he's been an asshole lately."

I wanted to ask her what she meant by sponsor. Was he her mentor in a drug rehabilitation program? Her sugar daddy? A client of some sort?

But the question seemed inappropriate, as did all the others I wanted to ask. I wasn't sure yet if the sex thing was really on—if she had also been informed that she was going to deep throat me tonight—and didn't quite know how to confirm the appointment.

Leslie wasn't the type of girl I normally slept with, or even talked to. Experienced would be a polite way to describe her face, which was a weird shade of red—not from the sun, but from some style of makeup application I'd only seen used by bag ladies on public buses. She had teeny teeth pressed close together, which would have been cute if they weren't out of proportion to her broad face, sabotaging every smile.

Her body, however, was glorious. She was a big girl. Not fat, but solid. Mighty would be a better word. Her pink-powdered breasts heaved out of her dress, daring you not to look at them. Her thighs were thick and muscular, and looked like they could perform all sorts of functions on construction sites. And her posture screamed sexuality and multiple orgasms. You could tell by the way her back arched away from the seat and thrust the full force of her tremendous chest into the steering wheel.

This was all so exotic to me. Though I tell girls I weigh 140 pounds, I've actually never been able to get above 126, no matter how much I eat or work out. Until recently, I had only dated really small women with low self-esteem, because that was all I could handle. This girl was an Amazon, a really trashy one, possibly even a real-life whore. It doesn't get any worse than that. And worse is what I'm all about.

When we arrived at the hotel, she reached behind her seat, grabbed a small overnight bag, and brought it with her into the hotel. As soon as I saw this, I knew Justin had made good on his promise.

I just had one major concern left.

"So, what are you doing for work these days?" I casually asked during dinner.

"I used to be a dancer," she said, "but now I'm between jobs."

As we talked further, I tried to pull more details from her. The best I could gather was that she'd been a stripper for six years, made a few adult films, and now used certain former clients for shelter, gifts, and travel. I suppose that makes her a prostitute, just as much as it makes any woman who dates or marries for money one.

After dinner, we took the elevator to my room. There still hadn't been a word or gesture of intimacy between us. Even though she was doing this for blood and not for money, there was something unsettling about the whole arrangement. Some guys enjoy having sex as a transaction, rather than an act of passion. But I get my rocks off as much through connection and, on a shallower level, validation as through the friction of flesh. I need to know that the woman I'm with wants to be with me because she genuinely likes me as a person—whether it takes three minutes or three years for her to come to that decision—or else the mutual surrender so key to the transgressive pleasure of sex never happens.

I decided to take some time to connect with her before the deep throating commenced.

"If you had to choose one thing in the world that makes life worth living, what would it be?" I asked as we walked in the room.

"Hmm," she said, nodding her head and pulling off her dress. Still thinking, she unhooked her bra. Her breasts were gargantuan. I could have placed a dictionary between them and they'd hold it like bookends.

She knelt in front of me and began unbuckling my belt.

We can always connect afterward, I decided.

"Why don't you stand in front of the bed?" she suggested as I stepped out of my pants.

I complied, as if following a nurse's instructions for a physical. She climbed onto the bed, rolled over, and dropped her head backward over the edge of the bed. I realized that this must be her special trick.

I stood in front of her and approached her open mouth with my dick in the air. It felt like some sort of carnival game.

She brought her hands up, wrapped them around me, and nudged me into her. Then she began adjusting her head in small movements, guiding me into her throat like a maze, until her mouth was at my base.

Euphoria swept through my body. In that moment, I knew my answer to the question I'd asked when we walked in the room.

She began sliding me back and forth inside her, slowly at first, clamping her throat and lips around me every time she hit bottom. Glancing down, all I could see were her outstretched neck and chin and, for some reason, they reminded me of the belly of a penguin. It was solely due to this image that I was able to refrain from orgasm and proceed to intercourse.

"I want to bring a girl out with us tomorrow," Leslie said, greedily puffing on a cigarette afterward. "She's got a gorgeous body. I've been trying to get with her for years. Maybe you can help me out."

My uncle used to warn me, "When pigs become hogs, they get slaughtered." I was about to ignore his advice and try to arrange a foursome.

"That would be cool," I told Leslie. "I was actually thinking about bringing along this Iranian girl I know who wants to learn Tantric sex. I told her you were a guru, so maybe you can show her a few things after dinner."

"Or during dinner." She smiled, exposing her teeny teeth. I couldn't imagine a weirder partner in crime. I was actually starting to like her, which was a good thing, considering that I'd just slept with her.

The following evening, after Leslie and I finished another game of penguin, there was a light, rapid knocking on the door. I opened it to find a woman with long legs encased in tight jeans, a flat, exposed abdomen, and a half-shirt clinging to large natural breasts.

Her face, however, was etched in permanent frown lines, stamped with dark circles around the eyes, framed in an explosion of frantic black hair, and crowned by a halo of drama. This was Samantha.

The first words out of her mouth were: "I need to borrow your phone."

Leslie's friend, Leslie's problem.

She took Leslie's phone, shut herself in the bathroom, and yelled at someone's answering machine as the bellhop arrived with three black bags. Samantha was moving in.

I left the room for the temporary refuge of the lobby and called Farah to warn her that my friends were going to be a little unusual. When I returned, Leslie was wearing a leopard-print dress with a plunging neckline and Samantha had changed into an imitation fur vest with nothing underneath.

When we walked through the lobby, a skinny bald guy sandwiched between two curvy giants dressed like eighties streetwalkers, every head turned. For a moment, I thought this was all a practical joke Justin was playing on me, but he's too broke to hire girls. Just to be safe, on the cab ride to the restaurant, I checked Leslie's ID to make sure she shared Justin's last name. Fortunately, her credentials checked out.

"I lost my credit card," Samantha prattled. "Do you guys mind if I borrow money just for tonight?"

"You're on your own, kid," I told her. I wasn't going to let her put me in the daddy role. If she wanted respect, she'd have to earn it.

Farah was waiting for us at the restaurant in a black strapless evening dress. She far outclassed my company.

"This is Leslie, the Tantra teacher I told you about," I said.

Farah smiled and greeted her. Only a slight, involuntary furrow down the center of her forehead gave away her befuddlement as to how this pink-boobed leopard woman could possibly be a spiritual guru.

The maître d' led us to a table in the outdoor garden, where a movie was being projected onto the wall. Conveniently, the film was *Last Tango in Paris.*

To break the ice, I ordered a bottle of wine and performed a few illusions I'd recently learned, including one where I cause a ball of paper to rise off the table and float into the air.

"If he can send his energy to objects, imagine what he can do with parts of your body," Leslie told Farah. She was a great wing.

"That stuff scares me," Samantha interjected. Every word out of her mouth was a plea for sympathy. "I need more wine. Can someone get the waiter over here? I think I'm getting a migraine."

The meal was interminable. No matter what subject we discussed, Samantha managed to bring it back to her neuroses. If we were talking about the movie on the wall, she complained that her cable was out and the repairman wouldn't come over. If we were discussing sex, she complained that the guy she was dating hadn't called her all week. If we were exchanging stories about nights out in London, she went on a tirade against her brother because he's a travel agent and never gets her deals.

My head ached just listening to her. "Do you see a pattern?" I finally snapped. "Your repairman won't come over, your boyfriend doesn't call you, and your brother doesn't help you out. Maybe the problem isn't everybody else; maybe it's you."

Her face scrunched, her eyes puffed, and she fell quiet for the remainder of the meal. I could tell that she was adding the comment to her archive of victim stories to tell for sympathy.

I'd just destroyed the night's foursome. And I was fine with that. It wasn't worth the headache. After dinner, I told Leslie and Samantha that I was going to a party with the Iranian princess. They seemed fine with that, and said they were going to a dance club.

However, between the magic tricks I'd performed, which led Farah to think I had actual shamanistic powers, and the company I kept, which led her to think I had a perverted sex life, she kept her guard up. When she dropped me off at the hotel after the party, we made out tepidly in the car. She seemed to be accepting my kisses, rather than returning them.

I walked to the elevator, dejected. My foursome had turned into just me, alone, again. My uncle was right. When pigs become hogs, they get slaughtered.

When I stepped off the elevator, I saw Leslie, Samantha, and a third girl I didn't recognize smoking in the hallway and waiting to get in the room. I'd assumed they'd be out partying all night.

Their friend introduced herself as Dee. She was petite, with a quiet confidence and braided hair extensions that ran halfway down her body. Her skin seemed Latin American, her facial features Native American, her backside African American.

Inside the room, Dee pulled a water bottle out of her purse, took a sip, and handed it to Leslie. Leslie took a small swig, then handed it to me.

"GHB," Samantha warned.

I passed it back to Leslie unsipped. I officially owed Samantha one.

Leslie fished into her overnight bag and produced a metallic green dress with an oval cutout running from just below the neck to the navel. "Hey, you have to try this on," she said to Samantha. I admired Leslie's talents as an instigator.

Samantha emerged from the bathroom moments later, looking like a Christmas tree with a misshapen star. "This one's perfect for you, Dee," Leslie said, pulling a white mesh minidress out of her bag.

Dee did not use the bathroom. She pulled off her jeans and tank top, revealing a body designed for the covers of muscle car magazines, and put on the dress.

"Mmm, you look good," Leslie purred. She walked up to Dee, laid a hand on the center of her chest, and began making out with her.

I was in the presence of a professional.

Within minutes, Dee was spread-eagled on the bed with her dress hiked up and Leslie's face between her legs. I sat next to them in my dinner clothes, not on GHB, thinking, This is cool.

When I joined them, via the nearest available breast, Leslie looked up at me, chin wet, and grinned from ear to ear. She reminded me of a coyote eating carrion.

"It's too hot in here," Samantha said suddenly. "I need some air."

By air, she meant attention. "Come join us," Leslie trilled, rising from the bed to bring Samantha into the mix.

"I want to clean the room a little first. You guys go on ahead. Don't mind me." The room wasn't even messy.

"Maybe I'll join you guys later," she added awkwardly, unconvincingly. "Looks like fun."

Leslie returned to the bed and pulled my clothes off. She and Dee both went down on me.

"Do you think there's an ironing board anywhere?" Samantha asked.

This was becoming even stranger than a foursome.

"You know what you can do?" I suggested, once again ignoring my uncle's advice. "Grab my camera off the table and take some photos."

Leslie and Dee didn't object; there probably wasn't much they'd object to. As the flashes went off, and the two of them earned their way into my shortlist of deathbed memories, I tried not to orgasm. A woman's sexual appetite, once unleashed, is much more voracious than a man's, and if I blew it now, I'd be stuck on the sidelines for the rest of the game.

"What button do you press to see the photos?"

I ignored her. This was my moment to shine.

"I'm bored," Samantha moaned. "I'm going to take a bath."

Leslie jumped up. "I'll help you."

Samantha was doing this on purpose.

Ten minutes later, Leslie returned from the bathroom, rebuked, and asked me to take a shot.

I grabbed a towel, wrapped it around myself, and sat on the edge of the bath.

Samantha was sitting naked in shallow water, her legs bowed out like a bratty child's.

"Everything okay?" I asked.

"Yeah, I'm okay. I like it here."

I decided to push my luck. It is my nature to push my luck. I am a hog.

I slipped off the towel and joined her in the bath. As we talked, I massaged her arms and legs. She didn't stop me.

I circled my fingers around her nipples until they hardened, then ran my tongue across them. She didn't stop me.

I moved my hand up her leg, until it reached the apex, and traced my finger slowly down her opening. She stopped me.

"No," she said, pushing my hand away. "Too much."

I'd been so worked up from the activity in the bedroom that I'd neglected to turn her on enough. And that was fine. Two birds in the bed, I decided, are better than one in the bathtub. I'd have to share that aphorism with my uncle next time I saw him.

When I returned, Dee was going down on Leslie. I joined her, and eased my finger up to her G-spot. This was more like it.

Leslie moaned and arched her back. She shuddered to orgasm, then begged us to keep going. Dee and I switched positions, and Leslie quaked again. She begged for more. For what seemed like forty-five minutes, she kept us down there, giving her orgasm after orgasm. My jaw ached, my wrist hurt, I began thinking about how good a Caesar salad with huge seasoned croutons would taste. Leslie kept arching her back, making us work harder and harder for each orgasm. But, as greedy as she was, I didn't stop. I wanted to show my appreciation for what she'd arranged tonight.

"Wow, that bath felt so nice." The fun-ruiner had returned. "Do you guys mind if I call room service? I'm hungry."

"No," I told her. The last thing we needed was room service busting in on the action.

"No, you don't mind or no, I shouldn't do it?"

"No, now would be a bad time."

Leslie, somehow, managed to have another orgasm during all this.

"I'm just going to make some tea."

I don't care.

I put on a condom, made sure it was unrolled to the very bottom, then entered Dee while she was going down on Leslie.

"Oh, here's the ironing board."

She must be on crystal meth.

"Do you mind if I iron your shirt?"

I may be all about worse, but this was becoming a nightmare. It was like having sex with my mother in the room.

Eventually, both Samantha and Dee were satisfied and they fell asleep. Not even a thank-you.

"You can go to bed now," I told Samantha. "You're safe."

"That's okay," she said, sitting in the desk chair. "I'm an insomniac."

Definitely meth.

With my mind and heart still racing from the night's adventure, I had trouble falling asleep. Samantha, conscious of this, began reciting her life story—her father shooting himself in front of the family at a dinner party; her mother leaving her at an aunt's house and never coming back; her first love beating her throughout the ten years they dated.

No wonder she was always begging for help and attention: Everyone she loved had left her or abused her. And, decades later, she was still searching for the safety she'd never felt as a child. Thanks to the needy way she went about it, however, she ended up replaying her childhood rejections with every new person she met instead.

I actually began to feel bad for her. Then I fell asleep.

In the morning, I woke to the sensation of Dee biting my neck. We were the only ones in the bed. It felt kind of empty.

"Where's everyone else?"

"They're in the bathroom," she whispered.

She reached around and stroked me. "Do you have another condom?" she asked.

I put one on. She rolled onto her side, with her back to me, and I entered her. When I began to moan, she whispered for me to be quiet, as if worried Leslie would hear us. I couldn't understand why this was an issue. Maybe she thought I was Leslie's man. Maybe we were breaking some unwritten law of the ménage à trois. Or maybe she'd just forgotten to bring her dildo that morning.

An hour later, we packed our bags, left the room, and took the walk of shame through the busy hotel lobby. Samantha offered to drive me to the airport and, as the four of us waited for her car at the valet stand, she grabbed my hand.

"Your skin is so soft," she said coquettishly. This was so out of her character that I didn't know how to respond.

Her car was not old and sleek like Leslie's. Just a beat-up white Malibu from the nineties. Its dented body, grinding brakes, neglected interior, and broken taillight conveyed nothing but hard living and bad luck.

After she pulled up to the terminal, Samantha applied lipstick, pulled an envelope out of her purse, and covered it with kisses. Then she handed it to me. I took a last look at the women in the car. I was actually going to miss them.

I guess I had connected with Leslie after all—and, as much as I was loath to admit it, with Samantha, as well.

As I flew back to the relative normalcy of home, I opened the envelope. Inside was a torn scrap of paper covered front and back with tiny scrawl:

> *Please call me next week or e-mail me. You turned me on very much, and I haven't felt what you had me feeling in a long time. It was a relaxing, sexual feeling. A turn-on that I never felt. I would have liked to experience being with you! I think you're a wonderful guy. I want to thank you for making me feel the way you did, and you didn't even know that you did. I sure wanted to suck your dick.*

The next day, I loaded the photos she had taken onto my computer. They were the most compromising images I'd ever been in:

I could actually see Leslie's insides for several layers. It would be a disaster if they ever leaked on the Internet.

I opened a secure deletion program to wipe them off my computer forever. And then I sat there, listening to my hard drive grind out 0s and 1s, until the night never existed. They were from another world. And I had fit into that world a little too well.

RULE 6
EXPECT THE BEST,
PREPARE FOR THE WORST

Dear Stacy,

You write the best e-mails. They are so thoughtful, warm, and tender. I wonder sometimes what it would be like to kiss you. I imagine that you would fully give yourself with a kiss, that it would be, like your e-mails, thoughtful and tender. I think of the warmth of your mouth, the joy of the first intimate touch, and how at first you might be a little nervous, but as you relax into the feeling, you would get lost in the moment, and our bodies, time, and the rest of the world would just melt away into that one single kiss.

Good night, Stacy. I hope all is well.

—Neil

P.S. I was pleased to hear that John and your sister are engaged. Please pass on my congratulations, and my gratitude to them for introducing us.

Dear Neil,

Your description of our kiss leaves me rather speechless. I can definitely feel the nervousness at first, but then the love pours in as we embrace. I don't want to sound corny, but that simply is how I envision our kiss: like the sun, love just warms everything about us.

I should warn you of something, though: I am a novice when it comes to kissing and sexuality in general.

Here's the short version of the story: for many years, I have battled anorexia nervosa, and because of my low weight over a period of time, my sexual experience remained at zero. Only recently have I begun to branch out and respond to sexual stimuli, which makes me a late bloomer at twenty-eight.

The next time I see you, I may be a bit heavier than I was in Chicago. I seem to have overcome the disease in the last few months. Well, not completely, but let's just say I've eaten a lot of chocolate chip cookies lately!

So, I do not mean to shock you, but that is my story. I am a very loving person, and I have so much love to give, but my knowledge of love-making is about minus ten. But wouldn't it be fun to learn, and start with the most beautiful kiss of the century?

When can we see each other and fulfill the wish? I can surely swing a visit to L.A., but only if you're willing to have me after all I've divulged in this message.

Keep enjoying yourself and write back soon.

Yours,
Stacy

Dear Stacy,

I'm writing this from Australia. I arrived safely yesterday, and wanted to thank you as soon as possible for sharing your story with me.

I don't want to make you wait, wondering what I'm thinking. So I will let you know now that I truly appreciate your candor and honesty. I would never think any differently about you as long as you are making progress. So you can put those worries to rest. I promise to be a patient teacher. If you're a really good girl, I'll even buy you some chocolate chip cookies.

I remain willing and eager to have you visit, and see all the places I've been telling you about. How does February 21 to 24 work for you?

E-mail me your address, and I'll send you a postcard and show you the beach on the Gold Coast where I surfed today. I miss you, too. Funny, huh, considering that we've only spent a total of ninety minutes together?

—Neil

Dear Neil,

I really have no special reason to write: just wanted to chitter-chat with you since I am so exceptionally fond of you (on some level, let's face it: I love you). Right now I am looking at icicles the size of lances hanging off the eaves of our roof, and I am thinking of you on the Gold Coast surrounded by gold. Gold: the alchemy that we create, you and I, together.

Send me messages—messages full of your joy and love and whatever you have to spare. If you need to vent, put it here. If you need to wax ebullient, put it here. If you need to say a cuss word, put it here. If you need anything, put it here. You are guaranteed a reception and a proper response. Just because I care so deeply for you.

In the meantime, just know that my crush keeps getting bigger every day. By the time I visit you on the 21st, I'll have pummeled you into the ground with my crushing affection. Hope you don't mind!

Love,
Stacy

Dear Stacy,

Apologies for the delay. Thank you again for another beautiful e-mail. I look forward to your visit, and want to assure you that I have no expectations of you or for anything to happen, just like I hope that you have no expectations of me. I must admit that I worry about your crush: I hope that I can live up to it. Looking forward to next week. Expect to see me waiting for you at the baggage claim. I'll be the one carrying the tray of chocolate chip cookies.

—Neil

Dear Neil,

Thank you for a lovely trip to Los Angeles. I had an unforgettable time exploring the Getty Museum with you, and it was a thrill learning to surf.

While I am disappointed that things didn't work out for us, I will savor forever the alchemy of our kisses and my first sexual explorations.

I am of course aware that gradually you distanced yourself from me, and I apologize for my lack of sexual experience and *my crushing affection and everything else that probably scared you away. Because of my condition, I am not as comfortable with myself as I'd like to be.*

I think you are a special person, and I will always have a space in my heart for you. Thank you again for showing me your world.

I am sad, but I will pray for you.

Love,
Stacy

Dear Stacy,

It was great to see you. And I feel the same way. You write the most beautiful e-mails I've ever received, and I will treasure them always.

I suppose an explanation is in order: I was so excited to see you at the airport, after all our e-mails, each one increasing in intensity. And, I must admit, at some point, I was a little scared, as well. When we went back to my house, I think reality set in. When I discovered that you still had your hymen, I realized you were no ordinary girl and this was no ordinary experience.

I didn't know if I could live up to your expectations, or ever reciprocate the immense reservoir of feeling you have for me. So I thought it would be better to back off and be friends, and let you have that other experience with the incredible person you're really supposed to be with. I can be a great lover, but I've always been a horrible love. I don't know if it's an emotional failing of mine, or if it's simply that our worlds are so different. You go to church every Sunday; I write books on Marilyn Manson.

You have so much love in your heart and goodness in your soul, and I'm glad that you were able to share just a little of it with me.

Are you familiar with Ryokan's poetry? The first part is by Ryokan and the second part is by Teishin. These are what I call good for the night poems.

Ryokan's letter:
Having met you thus
For the first time in my life,
I still cannot help
Thinking it but a sweet dream
Lasting yet in my dark heart.

Teishin's reply:
In the dreamy world,
Dreaming, we talk about dreams.
Thus we seldom know
Which is, and is not, dreaming.
Let us, then, dream as we must.

Good night, Stacy,
Neil

RULE 7
WHATEVER'S
IN THE WAY *IS* THE WAY

"I was at a friend of mine's house and this storm came up out of nowhere, man, with big clouds that looked like snakes standing up," he was saying, his deep voice reverberating off the hotel room walls. "I had one of those little twelve-dollar cameras in the glove compartment of my truck and I just snapped pictures. When I got the photos back, there was an image of God with his beard blowing in the wind, standing up in the storm."

He was one of the most important musicians of the century. After weeks of work, I had finally persuaded him to sit down for a two-hour interview. And everything was going well—until the last ten minutes. That was when his granddaughter walked in the room. Suddenly, I found myself unable to focus on a word he said.

She had thick black hair, long muscular legs, a high forehead, and tremendous breasts lifted high in her sweater. Her silhouette was the kind people made stencils out of and stuck on the mud flaps of trucks. Judging by her proud posture and haughty air, she seemed well aware of the effect she had on men. But, worst of all, she seemed bored.

She lounged on the bed, picking feathers out of the pillowcase. In her mind, I was just another white guy pumping her grandfather for trivia from fifty years ago.

I had to do something to change that.

"In my belief, there's a supreme being who can show himself whenever he feels like it. But he comes angry at the way we live and treat one another. He didn't mean for us to fight like cats and dogs. He meant for us to get along and love one another until death takes us away," he concluded.

"Let me ask you a question, since you understand human nature so well," I began. I needed to pull his granddaughter into the conversation: "You can help out, too, if you want."

She glanced up indolently, mildly interested. "You know how they say women are more attracted to power and status than looks?" I continued, beginning an admittedly ridiculous opener I'd been testing lately to start conversations with women. "I was talking to a friend about it the other day and he asked a good question: 'Then why is it that most women would rather sleep with Tommy Lee than George Bush? Isn't George Bush one of the most powerful men in the world?' "

"Who's Tommy Lee?" he asked.

"He's the heavy metal drummer who did that sex tape with Pamela Anderson," his granddaughter explained.

"Well, that tells you something right there," he said. "It's because rock 'n' roll is soulful. You listen to it to get away from all that political bullshit."

"George Bush is ugly," the granddaughter opined, too beautiful to bother with the actual point of the question. "That's why no one wants to sleep with him."

Weak answers to a weak opener, but it had served its purpose: the focus of the conversation had now shifted to her.

"She wants to move here and model," he explained. "She's not like them toothpick girls. Skin and bones do not excite me. They need young girls with figures like Alicia's."

He wrestled his pocket for a mint, then shoved it in his mouth. "The burning went to the wrong place," he coughed.

This seemed to remind her that he was old and that time was short. She massaged his shoulders, waited for him to regain his composure, then made her agenda known: "Don't forget, you promised to take me shopping."

"This is her first time in New York," he went on, "but I reckon I'll be sorry I brought her."

These were all clues: model, shopping, new to city, Grandpa's reluctance to shop. Before I put these clues to use, there was one thing I still needed to know. "You're how old now and you've never been here?"

"Twenty-one," she replied.

The word granddaughter had worried me.

"She has to go to Century 21," I said, planting the seed to spend more time with her. "They sell every designer brand you can think of for practically nothing. She'll spend hours there."

After the interview, he decided to take a nap. I gallantly offered to take Alicia off his hands and escort her to Century 21.

She glided by my side through the streets, speaking rarely, smiling never. This was her first time in New York—dense with noise, drama, dirt, culture, chaos, life—and she was sleepwalking through it all. She seemed to exist in a glass box that separated her from the rest of the world. And I wanted, more than anything, to smash through it.

I once told the story of Sleeping Beauty to a young cousin of mine. "How can a prince fall in love with a girl who's sleeping?" she asked afterward.

"Good point," I replied. "She may be beautiful, but they haven't even spoken. What if she's a complete bitch?"

This is probably why relatives don't allow me around their kids.

At the time, I didn't have an answer for her. Now I did: He loves her simply because he has the power to wake her.

At Century 21, I tried to flirt with Alicia, choosing the ugliest outfits and insisting she try them on. But no matter what I did, I couldn't break through her reserve. She still saw me as an antique collector rummaging through the closet of her grandfather's mind.

She left the store two hours later with a purple satin dress, a lace skirt, and an extra-large men's polo shirt. The shirt, she said, was for her boyfriend.

This complication would have been much easier to take if the shirt had been a size that was easier to compete with. Like extra-small.

That night, I had plans to see a stylist I was sleeping with named Emily. I'd talked to her for a few minutes at a party once. Afterward, she found my e-mail address online, wrote to me, and suggested getting together for coffee.

"You're like heroin," she said when I arrived, late from shopping with Alicia. "All my friends say to stay away from you because I'm starting to fall in love with you."

When she pulled me into the bedroom and began undressing me, I imagined that her hands were Alicia's hands; I saw Alicia's mouth wrapped around me; I grabbed Alicia's thick black hair.

I had sex with Emily three times that night, and every time, I closed my eyes and imagined she was Alicia.

It was the most passionate sex Emily and I had ever had.

The following evening, after watching Alicia's grandfather perform, I went backstage to pay my respects and invite Alicia to a party at the Tribeca Grand Hotel that night. Slowly, languorously, as if she'd been asked to pass the sugar at the end of a long meal, she gave her consent: "Okay, pick me up at my hotel after I take Granddad back."

Because it was my last night in New York, and I didn't know whether or not Alicia would go out after the concert, I'd invited a date to the Tribeca Grand earlier that day. Her name was Roxanne. She was five foot two and one of the most sexual girls I knew.

An hour and a half after the show ended, Alicia emerged from her hotel, wearing the tight purple dress she'd bought. The cabdriver, the students across the street, some guy riding past on a bicycle all did a double take.

"I had to talk to my boyfriend," she said, apologizing for her tardiness. "We haven't spoken in like a week. He's so boring."

Sleeping Beauty was mine again to wake. Suddenly, extra-large meant nothing to me.

Roxanne was waiting for us in the lobby of the Tribeca Grand, wearing a spaghetti-strap top that exposed her little-doll back. She hugged me tightly, peering up through heavy black mascara. There was something mischievous in her eyes, her smile, her carriage that communicated she was willing to try anything anytime.

I had met Roxanne at a concert last time I was in New York. She worked part-time as a model for illustrators and had appeared on everything from biscuit tins to sex-position guides. Her boyfriend played drums in the small local band we were watching. And she invited me to the afterparty at the singer's apartment.

Roxanne, her boyfriend, and I spent most of the party lying on the host's bed, while he sat in a chair nearby. As Roxanne and I talked, her boyfriend rose to his feet, walked into the front room, and dragged a very drunk blonde onto the bed with us. Within seconds, he was making out with her. Two minutes later, he had her naked.

Roxanne didn't seem to mind, chiefly because she was too busy flirting with me: unnecessary touching, unsubtle innuendoes, unmistakable body language. Hesitantly, I took the bait. I looked over her shoulder as we kissed to see if her boyfriend minded. He was already fingering the drunk girl.

This is typically a sign of an open relationship.

I began making out with Roxanne more intensely. She grabbed me through my corduroys as her boyfriend began fucking the drunk girl. Some sort of jewelry glinted off his dick, rattling with each thrust. It was at this point that the singer left his own room.

As we fooled around, Roxanne kept glancing over at her boyfriend. She seemed upset, not necessarily because he was having sex with someone else, but because he was being inconsiderate of her while he did it.

She pulled down my pants and gave me an aggressive blow job. Then she grabbed a condom from her purse, slammed herself on top of me, and tried to outfuck her boyfriend. She ground herself vigorously against me, stuck a finger in her ass, and moaned loud enough to wake the whole building. This seemed to be how they fought.

It wasn't a good experience, but nobody ever said all experiences had to be good. Sometimes they're just experiences.

They broke up a few months later and, now that Roxanne was single, I was looking forward to sleeping with her under normal circumstances if things didn't work out with Alicia. Every single man needs a sexually adventurous woman he can count on to distract him from the fact that he is unloved.

"I brought some Ecstasy," Roxanne said after buying the first round of drinks at the Tribeca Grand. She pulled an orange pill bottle out of her purse and dumped a white tablet into her hand.

I'm not a fan of psychedelic drugs, mainly because they last too long. The word trip is appropriate: Like an airplane ride, there is no way to get off until you land. More important, I didn't think hugging a speaker for six hours would improve my chances with Alicia.

Pinching her teeny fingers together, Roxanne cracked the pill in two. One half instantly crumbled to pieces in her hand. Without even asking if I wanted it, she lifted the hand full of Ecstasy dust, clamped it over my mouth, and dumped the contents inside.

I tried to keep my cool, but my eyes widened in horror, as if they'd just seen the devil. I needed to find a way to keep from tripping. I couldn't just start spitting all over the club. So for the next five minutes, I kept bringing my glass of Jack and Coke to my lips and, instead of taking a sip, casually drooled the contents of my mouth into it. Then I went to the bathroom and poured the drink into the toilet. For the next hour, I was on edge, paranoid that the pill had absorbed into my bloodstream anyway.

Then I noticed Roxanne giving Alicia a massage on a couch upstairs. She'd already gotten further than I had with Sleeping Beauty. And that was fine with me, because it meant two things: The first was that I had succeeded in expelling the Ecstasy, because she was clearly in a drug-induced, tactile state and I still felt normal. The second was that a change of plans was in order. I might not have to choose between Roxanne and Alicia after all.

"My friend Steven has a great loft where I'm staying," I told them when their rubdown ended. "He and his roommates usually have parties every night, so we should see what's going on."

Roxanne, Alicia, and I took a cab to Steven's house, detouring at a corner deli to buy supplies: a bottle of Cabernet, Sun Chips, and turkey sandwiches on stale bread.

Inside the loft, the party had long since ended. Not only were Steven and his roommates sleeping, but two other guys were crashed out on couches in the living room. Unfortunately, I didn't have my own room. I had been sleeping on a futon on the floor across from the couches.

Roxanne and I sat on the guest futon. Alicia took a seat at a breakfast table a few feet away, unwrapped a turkey sandwich, and casually began eating it. I admired her ability to remain unaffected no matter where she went and what she saw. However, I was running out of time. There had to be some way to break the glass box in case of emergency.

"Hey," I whispered to Alicia, trying not to wake the two guys sleeping on the couch. "I have to show you the coolest video before you go."

My best wingman is my laptop.

She walked to the futon and perched on the edge with her arms wrapped around her knees. I showed her a clip of a species of bird that actually moonwalks across tree branches. I probably oversold the video, but it served its purpose, getting her on the futon.

It was now time to kiss Sleeping Beauty. Otherwise, she would return to the hotel and actually go to sleep.

I told Alicia and Roxanne that I'd recently had an amazing experience where two masseuses worked on me at the same time, in perfect synchronization. This procedure was known as the dual-induction massage, and I'd used it many times to segue into a threesome.

First, Alicia and I gave Roxanne a massage. Then I took off my shirt and they massaged me. Finally, I told Alicia to lower the top of her dress and lie on her stomach.

Typically, during the dual-induction massage, the energy in the room begins to shift and the inevitability of a safe, fulfilling, three-way sexual experience begins to dawn on everyone.

But this time, there was no shift in energy. Rather than relaxing into the touch and the sexual possibilities, Alicia lay there and quietly accepted the massage. Running my hands down the smooth, broad expanse of her back was as satisfying as it was frustrating, like smelling fresh bread in a locked bakery. I began to worry that she was politely waiting for her opportunity to leave, thinking we were some kind of creepy swinger couple who did this all the time.

Afterward, Alicia rose off the futon, pulled her dress up, and went to the bathroom. She didn't seem happy. She didn't seem upset. She didn't seem much of anything.

At least I'd tried. I was fooling myself by thinking Roxanne and I were Prince and Princess Charming anyway; we were more like the villains she needed to be rescued from.

"What do you suppose Alicia's thinking right now?" I asked Roxanne.

"I have no idea."

"Let's just check out her vibe when she comes back from the bathroom. And if she's not down, we'll put her in a cab."

Alicia returned from the bathroom to her perch on the edge of the futon, as if waiting to be dismissed. I'd definitely pushed her too far.

"Well, you should get some sleep before your trip tomorrow, so let's find you a cab."

She laid down next to me, hugged me good-bye, and said, "Thanks."

In the moment she hugged me, I sensed it was on. The energy shift I'd been waiting for had occurred.

I raced toward her lips, worried that if I hesitated for even a second, she'd be out the door. She melted into me. I could feel the glass box heating and cracking beneath my touch, falling off her skin in large panes. Faint murmurs of pleasure bubbled up through her lips.

Roxanne lay on the bed behind me. I turned around, pulled

her close, and made out with her. Then we began massaging and licking Alicia's breasts through her dress. Alicia lazily raised her arms, signaling that she was ready for it to be taken off.

Alicia was not a giver, but she was a great receiver. Her back arched and her hips flexed, showing off a body so perfect that all the owner had to do was possess it to be a good lover.

When I removed Alicia's panties, she was drenched. I ran to my suitcase, dug for a condom, and returned to the bed. I positioned both girls on their backs and entered Alicia as I made out with Roxanne. Then I entered Roxanne and made out with Alicia.

To my surprise, the girls didn't hesitate once, even though there were two guys sleeping—or pretending to sleep—on couches in full view of the action. One of my friends, when he's having sex with a beautiful woman, thinks, I deserve this. I kept thinking, I can't believe this is happening to me. Are they blind?

A swinger couple I know used to tell me about their three-somes and, with delight and wonder in his eyes, the man would talk about his favorite position: the triangle.

The time had come to experience the legendary triangle. I lay on my back, and told Alicia to ride me. Then I had Roxanne sit on my face, opposite Alicia, so the two of them could make out.

However, I never felt the cosmic sexual flow my friend used to talk about. Instead, I felt blind and smothered. Roxanne was sitting on my eyes.

Not that I'm complaining.

Afterward, Alicia spoke first. "That's the first time I ever did anything like that," she said quietly.

"You mean a threesome, or being with a girl?" I assumed she wasn't talking about the triangle.

"Both," she said.

"How do you feel?"

"It was . . ." She paused. ". . . good."

She was never much for words.

Alicia and I stayed in touch after that. We had long phone conversations, during which her glass walls continued to fall away, exposing a goofy personality and wry sense of humor.

"Grandad likes you," she said one night. "He wants you to come visit us at home."

A week later, I flew in to spend the weekend and continue the interview in a setting few journalists ever got to see. Alicia picked me up at the airport and we drove to his home.

"I don't do this for just anyone," he said in his barreling voice when I arrived.

During the day, I watched him work in the studio. That night, Alicia snuck into my bed.

The next morning, at 6, her grandfather burst in the room. He took a look at us cringing under the sheets, then said to her, "I knew you were black-topping Neil."

He let out a loud, playful laugh, then turned to me. "Come outside, I want to show you something."

I followed him through the house and out the door. We stood in the grass and he pointed to the dawn sky. "Right there," he said. "What do you see?"

"Clouds."

"Look closer, man. What do you see in the clouds?"

They looked like smoke puffs, but he seemed so excited I didn't want to let him down. "God?" I asked.

"Yeah, God," he said, pointing at a thick wisp of cloud extending high into the sky. "You can never tell what He has in store for you. He moves in mysterious ways."

"Yes," I told him. "He definitely does."

RULE 8
EMOTIONS
ARE REASON ENOUGH

I've made a horrible mistake.

I got drunk and may have married someone the other night.

And now I'm worried I'll never see her again. Or maybe I'm worried that I will see her. I'm not sure which would be worse.

I don't know her age, where she lives, or her last name.

Well, I suppose I know her last name now.

I'm not the type to blame other people for my mistakes, but if I had to point a finger, it would be at Ragnar Kjartansson. All you need to know about him are two things: One, he's the singer in Iceland's only country band. Two, he's the first male ever to graduate from Husmadraskolinn, a school for housewives.

He is my tour guide here in Reykjavík, the capital of Iceland, and I don't mind saying that he's not a very good one.

The night in question began at Tveir Fiskar, which either means Two Fish or Three Raincoats, depending on what time of day you ask Ragnar. It's one of the only places where they serve whale steak and whale sushi in Iceland. They also serve rancid shark, which is best eaten in bite-size pieces and washed down by a shot of Black Death. The former tastes like belly-button lint, the latter like Windex.

"We must drink," Ragnar slurred, handing me my third shot of Black Death, "to being pathetic."

He had been on a bender for months, ever since his girlfriend, Disa, left him and took the TV. Without the TV to distract him, he explained, all he did was think about her.

"I should have married her," he went on, bobbing his head into mine. "You only get one chance at perfect love."

After dinner, as Ragnar struggled to pull a red wool sweater over his head, he suggested, "Let's go drinking."

"Isn't that what we've been doing all night?"

"That wasn't drinking. I'll show you drinking, the Iceland way."

Evidently, drinking the Iceland way meant vomiting under a table, urinating on a bus, getting in a fight with a teenager, and passing out in a crosswalk. Because that's exactly what Ragnar did over the course of the next three hours.

"Get up." I nudged him. It was October in the frozen north and he was wearing just a sweater. "You're going to die out here."

"Go on without me," he mumbled. "The bars of Reykjavík need you."

Even in his drunken stupor, he was trying to make me laugh. I hoisted him to his feet and brought him to the safety of the sidewalk. And that's when I saw the girl I would marry that night.

She was accompanied by some twenty tourists, all of whom were attending Iceland Airwaves, a music festival I was in town to write about. I recognized a photographer in the group and stopped to talk.

He introduced me to his friends. The only word I remembered was "Veronika."

She reminded me of the new wave singers I used to fantasize about in the eighties. She was petite, with spiky black hair, heavy blue eye shadow, laughing eyes, and full lips parted slightly to expose a perfect row of white. As soon as I saw her, I was smitten.

"Is he going to be okay?" she asked, gesturing to Ragnar.

"Yes, he's heartbroken."

"I wish my heartbreaks were like that."

"Yeah, he does look pretty happy for a guy who's lost his perfect love."

"I've never had perfect love," she said. "I wouldn't even know how to recognize it."

"You don't have to recognize it. You just know."

One of the things I've learned from traveling with rock bands—besides how to play FIFA World Cup soccer on a moving bus, survive without showering for seven days, and sleep inches away from five people who also haven't showered for seven days—is that groups move at the speed of their slowest member. And, considering that most of Veronika's friends were drunk, they weren't going anywhere soon. So I suggested slipping away, finding something interesting to do, then rejoining them in a little while.

"What about Loverboy?" she asked, gesturing to Ragnar.

"He can be our third wheel. Every date needs one."

She looked at her friends, then smiled her consent. We backed away wordlessly, with Ragnar wobbling behind us.

"*It's hard to be loved,*" he began singing. "*Baby, I'm unappreciative.*"

"No wonder she broke up with him." Veronika laughed. I liked her. In order to be alone with her, however, I'd have to dismiss my hapless tour guide. I knew he'd understand—or, more likely, forget. So I flagged a taxi and stuffed him inside.

As I closed the door, he grabbed the bottom of my jacket. "Don't say no to love," he slurred. "Or you will be pathetic like me."

"I feel bad for him," Veronika said as he sped away.

"Don't feel bad for him. Being pathetic is an art form to him. He comes from a very accomplished family, so he distinguishes himself by being hopeless at everything: the worst drunk, the worst country singer, the worst boyfriend, the worse housewife."

"I suppose there's a sort of dignity there," she said.

Downtown Reykjavík on a weekend night is a combat zone, with bottles smashing against walls, cars careening onto sidewalks, and hordes of drunk teenagers zigzagging the streets. There's no malevolence in the air, like after a rugby game in England, just an absence of control.

Veronika and I found refuge in a small line outside the door of an after-hours club. She was from the Czech Republic and had been living in New York City for the last year. That was all I managed to learn before a guy with an unbuttoned overcoat, spiky brown hair, and a smooth face ruddy from the cold staggered in line behind us. He had a backpack slung on one shoulder and a big alcoherent smile on his face.

"Okay, okay," he blurted, barreling into our conversation. "From where do you reside?"

"The States," I replied curtly.

"It is beautiful for spacious skies," he said earnestly, as if he had just spoken magic words that would win him the approval of any American. "And may I ask as to whether you are male friend and female friend?"

"We actually just got engaged tonight," I said, hoping that would extinguish any hope he had of hitting on Veronika.

"That is blessed news." He smiled sloppily. Most people in Reykjavík were nearly fluent in conversational English, but he spoke as if he'd learned the language from technical manuals, greeting cards, and parliamentary papers. "For what measure of time do you date?"

"Seven years," Veronika told him, playing along. "Can you believe it took him this long to step up? He's scared of commitment." Definitely a keeper.

"That's because she's always nagging me about the trash and the cigar smoking and my checkered past."

"I can help," the guy said. "I can help. My surname is Thor. And I will marry you in holy wedlock."

"That would be great," I told him. It seemed like the perfect opportunity to make a connection with Veronika.

"Okay, okay, I need ring for ceremony," Thor said. He swung his backpack under his shoulder and began digging through it. "You are sure?"

"It's my dream come true," Veronika said, sighing.

"Okay," Thor prattled on. "This will be okay." He scooped a bottle of vodka out of his backpack, unscrewed the cap, and worked furiously to remove the metal ring around the neck. It snapped apart.

"Wait, wait." Undeterred, he produced a cell phone from the bag and slid off a metal loop that appeared to be an empty key ring.

He seemed so intent, so determined, so excited. We enjoyed watching the show. It was as if he'd been sent by a higher power to keep us entertained and prevent the awkwardness that usually occurs when two people who like each other hang out for the first time.

He said something in Icelandic to two guys in line behind him and they moved into position on either side of him. Then he cleared his throat and began:

"Dearly beloved, we gather today under God and witnesses to join pleasing couple in bonds of holy matrimony, okay, okay. Pleasing couple, I forecast your happiness for infinity. Your love is like sun shining in morning. It makes light of world."

At first, I thought he was simply playing the clown to amuse us. But as he went on, he seemed to be struggling, with all the soberness and poetry he could muster, to make the moment meaningful.

After five more minutes of grandiloquent speech, he furtively pressed the key ring into my hands, then addressed me: "Do you take this woman to be your wife in holy wedlock? Do you guarantee to love, honor, and protect her until death parts you apart? Do you guarantee to love her and only her in wellness and in health, okay, okay?"

"Okay."

"Do you take this man to be your husband in marriage? Do you guarantee to do all the things I just speeched to him, okay, okay?"

"Okay."

"I now pronounce you man and wife," he intoned loudly. "You may kiss on the bride."

As Veronika and I made out, I welled up with gratitude to Thor, who was already busy pulling something else out of his backpack.

"I insist on pleasure of gifting you with first wedding gift, okay, okay," he said. He then handed us each a small crescent of chocolate wrapped in blue-and-silver foil and made another rambling, romantic speech full of okays.

We thanked him for the passion he had put into the ceremony. And he beamed, proud of himself, then reached again into his backpack and pulled out a pen and a notepad.

"Please give to me your mail address, okay, okay," he said.

We both complied, figuring that he wanted pen pals.

"Make sure you spell full names with correctness."

He folded the piece of paper and put it in his pocket, then nodded happily and announced: "I will send certificate of marriage in mail, okay, okay."

I blanched for a moment, then realized he probably just meant a greeting card. He'd definitely gotten carried away with the whole charade. "What do you mean?" I asked, just to make sure.

"I am priest, of course," he said, as if it had been obvious the whole time. "I have certification with church. It is okay. We accept all religions."

Veronika and I both looked at each other, the same thought running through our minds: What have we just done?

Yet, oddly, neither of us told him not to prepare the certificates. He was so proud of himself, like a child who's taken his first shit on a grown-up toilet, that we didn't want to disappoint him. If he really was a priest, which he kept insisting, then it was too late anyway.

Once inside the club, we bought our priest a beer in exchange for his services, then snuck away to make out in the upstairs lounge. It was the most romantic first date of my life—and hopefully not the last first date.

There was little point in hanging out at the club, since we had no interest in talking to anyone else, so we left to find more adventure.

When we turned the corner, we saw Veronika's friends still standing on the sidewalk, exactly where we'd left them. We talked to them for a few minutes, but the conversation was awkward. They'd been standing there, doing nothing, while we'd been through so much. Our lives had, quite possibly, completely changed. So, once more, we slipped away.

She placed her hand softly in mine and we walked to the Hotel Borg like a couple on honeymoon. Upstairs, we collapsed onto the bed. It seemed obvious where this all was leading.

So obvious that, for the first time all night, Veronika began to get nervous.

"I've had the best time," she said between kisses.

My heart raced. I felt the same way. She continued: "This night is just too perfect. It can't be real."

We kissed again. Then: "I have to go."

And then: "This is too much."

Finally: "I knew you were going to try to do this."

It was clear what was going on. The specter of sex had cast gender roles on us. I was a man, moving toward pleasure, and she was a woman, moving away from pain. The same fear men have of approaching women, most women have of going past the point of sexual no return with men.

And this is not just because of the biological repercussions—

pregnancy, labor, childbirth, nursing—but because most women have at some point been hurt by a man. So, before they risk giving themselves over to powerful emotions they have little control over, they want to make sure they're with someone who is being honest with them, respects them, and can reciprocate what they have to give—whether for a night or a lifetime. What many women secretly want is to throw themselves into the fire when they feel love without getting burned, scarred, or hurt. However, until scientists invent an emotional condom, it is typically the role of the man to reassure her before, during, and after that she's making the right choice. Not with logic, but with feeling.

"Before you leave," I told Veronika, "I'd like to tell you a story."

The story is not my own. It is about a man and a woman who randomly pass each other on the street one day. Both immediately get the intuition that the other is the one-hundred-percent perfect person for them. And, through some miracle, they work up the courage to speak to each other.

They walk and talk for hours, and get along perfectly. But, gradually, a sliver of doubt creeps into their hearts. It seems too good to be true. So, to make sure they're really supposed to be together, they decide to part without exchanging contact information and let fate decide. If they run into each other again, then they will truly know that they are each other's one-hundred-percent perfect love and will marry on the spot.

A day passes, a week passes, a month passes, years pass—and they don't see each other. Eventually, they each date other people, who are not their true love. Many years later, they finally pass on the street again, but too much time has gone by and they don't recognize each other.

"You see," I told Veronika afterward, "the lovers were lucky that fate allowed them to find each other once. When they doubted their feelings, it was like tearing up a winning lottery ticket and waiting for another one just to make sure they were really meant to win."

Afterward, there was silence. The metaphor had sunk in. We spent the night together talking about nothing but enjoying every word, fooling around but not having actual sex. Now I was not only indebted to Thor for the marriage, I was indebted to the Japanese writer Haruki Murakami for the honeymoon.

In the morning, as I lay in a state of semiconsciousness, Veronika kissed me good-bye. Rekyjavík is a small city and we were both attending the same concerts, so we promised to find each other the next night. I spent the afternoon daydreaming about her and about our unexpected connection.

That night, we went to Gaukar a Stong, one of Iceland's oldest pubs. As seemed to happen every night here, the strong alcohol, the hallucinatory music, the clear air, and the winsome populace seized hold of me, and I gave myself over to the adventure the city had in store for me.

It began as I was ordering another Egil beer. A woman's voice to my right asked, "Are you American?"

I turned around to see a lightly freckled girl with short platinum hair dressed in combat boots, torn stockings, and a black sweatshirt emblazoned with a silver lightning bolt.

The conversation quickly turned to stories of sexual adventures, and she began talking about an orgy she had recently experienced. It soon became clear that the intent of the story was not just to share but to arouse.

It worked.

As we made out at the bar, a woman tapped her on the shoulder. I pulled back to see Veronika standing there.

"I'm leaving the club now," she told the girl coldly. "You coming with?"

"Yes," the girl said, grabbing her purse off the counter. Then, to me: "My friend's usually not this rude. Sorry. Nice meeting you."

It all happened so fast and unexpectedly that I didn't have time to explain myself to Veronika. I had no idea she'd been in the bar the whole time, just as she had no idea I was there—until she saw me making out with her friend. I suppose there was nothing I could say to her anyway, other than she was right when she said that meeting me was too good to be true. I'd already hurt her.

And now I'm sitting on the flight from Reykjavík to Los Angeles, replaying every moment in my head. I have no idea how to find her—or if I'm actually married to her. All I have to remember her by is the blue-and-silver foil chocolate in the pocket of my jacket.

Days pass, weeks pass, months pass, and I never hear from her again. Yet I can't get her out of my mind. My allegory has backfired on me and I've somehow convinced myself that we're the living embodiment of the Haruki Murakami story.

I try to find her on MySpace, but there are too many Veronikas without profile pictures in New York. I track down the photographer who introduced us, but he doesn't know how to get in touch with her. And the promised marriage certificates never arrive, which is actually more a relief than a disappointment.

I keep the chocolate on my desk as a reminder of my guilt, of my susceptibility to my lower impulses, of the fact that it was I and not she who so recklessly tore up the lottery ticket we'd been given.

Then, one night a year later, on a trip to New York, I see her—my one-hundred-percent perfect girl. She is at Barramundi on the Lower East Side, sitting at a table and drinking with friends.

The words "It's my wife" burst out of my mouth. The conversation at the table stops and everyone wheels around to face me.

"Hubby," she shouts, a wide smile breaking over her face.

I join them, and the hours pass. Eventually, it's just the two of us again.

I've dated many girls since meeting her. And she tells me she's in a serious relationship. Yet we still get along perfectly.

"I'm sorry," I finally say, "about, you know, making out with your friend. That was really stupid of me. I've regretted it every day since."

"You're just a man." She sighs.

"Does that mean my behavior is excusable because of my gender, or you're disappointed because I acted like a typical guy?"

"I guess both." I watch her lips sip her cranberry and vodka. "I should tell you that I had a boyfriend when we met."

"Is that the person you're seeing now?"

"Yes. But it's not perfect love."

"Then why do you stay with him?"

"I guess—" she pauses, reflects, decides "—because it's convenient love."

An hour later, we find ourselves at the apartment where I'm crashing. I show her the dead pet goldfish my host, Jen, keeps wrapped in Saran Wrap in her freezer, and then, tired and tipsy, we fall asleep on the sofa bed.

In the morning, we have sex for the first time. It is perfect. We fall back asleep afterward in each other's arms.

When I wake up, she is gone. I search the living room, kitchen, and bathroom for a note. There is none. Once again, I have no way to reach her. And I have a feeling that's the way she wants it.

The problem with one-hundred-percent perfect love is that sometimes it's inconvenient.

Back in Los Angeles a month later, I give in to temptation. I've been working all night and there's nothing to eat in the house. I peel the blue-and-silver foil off the wedding present Thor gave us. Small discolored flakes of chocolate drop to the ground. The candy has turned brittle from age, lost its shape, and faded from brown to inedible gray. There is no point in keeping it anymore. It will only attract bugs.

RULE 9
LOVE IS A WAVE,
TRUST IS THE WATER

"I'm throwing up."

"Did you eat anything shady last night?" I ask her.

"No, I had what you did. How do you feel?"

"Fine, I guess."

"So."

This is where it begins to dawn on me that this is not a call for coddling. It is every unmarried man's nightmare—and many a married man's nightmare.

"Do you think you have food poisoning?" I ask. It's hard to just come out with the words. Their impact is too much to take.

"I don't know."

"Would you like me to get you some Emetrol?" I'm fishing now.

"Could you? Thanks." Pause. Wait for it. "And could you get a pregnancy test, too?"

When you know a slap across the face is coming, it actually hurts more.

I hang up the phone, brush my teeth, splash water on my face (an ex-girlfriend convinced me one morning that it's bad for the skin to use soap twice a day), and grab the car keys.

It is the worst trip a man has to make.

At the drugstore, I pick up crackers, ginger ale, and Emetrol antinausea medicine. Then I study the shelf of pregnancy tests. The E.P.T. Pregnancy Test seems the simplest: Pee on the white rod, then wait to see whether it displays a minus sign (indicating freedom) or a plus sign (indicating indentured servitude). I choose the kit with two test sticks. I may need a second opinion.

At the register, it is all too obvious what my errand is. This is far more embarrassing than buying condoms, though I imagine there are more humiliating things to buy. Like Preparation H. Or Valtrex. Or Vaseline and a plastic billy club.

They've probably seen it all.

I rush to Kathy's house. She answers the door wearing just a green T-shirt, her small face blanched, her blonde hair uncombed, her slender body beaded with perspiration. She looks great. No joke.

I unpack the groceries. The first thing she goes for is the ginger ale.

I carefully watch the pregnancy test to see if she's ready, but she just brings it into the bathroom with the medicine. Probably wants to wait. Too much to handle right now.

She doesn't mention it. Neither do I. She's already told me many times that she could never get an abortion. So there's no point in talking about it. Either we're screwed or we're not.

As she wanders around the house cleaning, I wonder how

we're supposed to administer the test. The best thing would probably be to go into the bathroom together, as a unit. I'll stand by her side, politely averting my head while she pees on the stick. Then we'll lay it on the countertop and wait. We can run through what-if scenarios together then.

I suppose I could marry her. When we first started dating, I thought she was the one. People say you just know, and for the first time I did: I remember making out with her on the couch on our second date and thinking, I love this girl, and knowing I'd have to wait at least a month before I could actually tell her. I remember watching her sleep, and realizing that I would always love her, no matter how old and wrinkly she gets.

But lately she's been jealous. She doesn't like it when I talk to other women at parties, even though I make it plain to them she's my girlfriend. She doesn't like it when I answer my cell phone when I'm with her, even if it's the middle of a weekday, we've been together seventy-two hours straight, and it's a work call. And when we're lying together and she's looking into my eyes and, for a second, I remember that I have to take my clothes out of the dryer, there's hell to pay for thinking of anything that's not her. I can't live for the rest of my life with the thought police.

This test better be negative.

She shuffles to the TV and puts in a DVD of *Sex and the City*, season three. She's seen every episode at least a dozen times. Refers to them often.

She always tells me that she will love me forever, but how can love exist without trust?

The anxiety affects my bladder like beer and I head to the bathroom. While washing my hands afterward, I notice the pregnancy stick lying on the countertop. She's got it just sitting there, ready to go. That's kind of sweet.

I pick it up and examine it. I've never actually studied one before. There's a little minus sign in the indicator window.

First thought: She's not pregnant. What a relief.

Second thought: She took the test without me?

I walk out of the bathroom to find her lying on the floor in front of the TV where I left her. She's watching the episode where Charlotte and Trey decide to take time apart.

"Why didn't you tell me it was negative?"

She looks up at me and shrugs, "I didn't want to bother you."

Then she turns back to the TV. I know how the episode ends. I know how all of them end. They'll break up. Then they'll get back together again. Then they'll break up again. Some things just aren't meant to be.

RULE 10
THE COMFORT ZONE
IS ENEMY TERRITORY

THE FIRST DAY

"Your balls are going to be in your throat and you'll be screaming in pain," she says.

"No," I tell her. "I can do it."

"Sure you don't want to wait a few more days?"

"I'll be fine. Now take off your pants."

Gina steps out of her pants and I lay her down on the couch. I want to make sure she's as close to orgasm as possible to make this easy on myself.

"No tricks, now," I warn as I enter her. "If I say stop, you have to stop."

It's different this way. I feel a sense of clarity I've never had during sex. My mind is alert and in the moment, instead of elaborately recording imagery to its fantasy database. I am detached from the friction and frisson, and as our grinding intensifies, my body begins to lighten and then dissolve.

She comes in slow, deep waves. Immediately afterward, she flails from side to side, as if the physical sensation is too much to take and she needs to crawl out of her skin until it subsides.

"I want to go surfing." These are the first words she says when she comes back to the present. She has not wanted to surf in two years, ever since her best friend died in the water. She looks like she's just seen the face of God.

I'm afraid it's the best sex she's ever had with me.

And it's all because I'm doing the 30 Day Experiment.

THE SECOND DAY

Linda calls and says she's in town. I haven't talked to her in two months. There must be some psychic signal I'm sending into the universe that says, "It's going to be really hard for me to have sex right now, so please come over and tempt me."

As soon as her lips touch mine, I'm hard. It is a different kind of hardness—urgent, independent, and definitely not going anywhere. She feels it and says, "I can always do that," as if she's responsible.

She says she doesn't want to have sex this afternoon, and that is fine. Just from the making out and rubbing, every nerve in my body is tensed and ready to explode. This gets more difficult each day.

I excuse myself to go to the bathroom, splash cold water on my face, and then return and tell her about the 30 Day Experiment.

That night, I talk to Kimberly on the phone. I'd messaged her on MySpace two weeks earlier. With her black bangs and large, innocent eyes, she reminded me of a Mark Ryden painting. She lives across the country in New York, but we've been talking nightly. She is easy to speak with, and the more I learn about her, the more I like her. Not only do we both collect 60's garage-rock and secretly enjoy being pushed around in grocery carts, but she is one of the sweetest, most genuine people I've ever never-met. Recently, I've been waking up thinking about her and randomly checking my phone throughout the day in case I miss a text from her.

I'd been wondering if she felt the same way about me. Tonight, I find out. After we hang up, she texts, "I'm rubbing my skin raw thinking about us. I hope you don't mind me admitting that to you."

I tell her that I don't mind and, six texts later, I know her favorite position, speed, and motion. While I'm having alphanumeric intercourse with Kimberly, Linda texts, "I want sex. Fuck your thirty days. Start it tomorrow."

Suddenly she's interested.

Then Kimberly texts, "My hips are moving so quick and high to meet my hand. I want to swallow you while I do it. Is that too much?"

Then Linda texts, "Baby, I want to fuck. Just one hour of bliss."

This kind of thing never happens.

Blood rushes to my pelvis. I feel like I'm going to pass out.

THE THIRD DAY

My friends think I've lost my mind. "Why put yourself through it?" they ask.

"Why does a man climb a mountain or walk on hot coals or read *Finnegans Wake*?" I answer.

I am doing it, first and foremost, to see if I can.

Rivers Cuomo, the singer and guitarist in Weezer, first planted the idea in my head. He was explaining that he'd recently taken a vow of celibacy as part of a Buddhist meditation program. This meant abstaining from not just sex but also masturbation. As a result, he said, he'd never felt more energized, creative, or focused in his life.

At the time, I interpreted it less as advice than as further confirmation of his peculiarities. But a few weeks later, Billy Corgan of the Smashing Pumpkins told me that he doesn't let his band have sex or orgasm on the day of a concert, so they can release all that power onstage.

Then, at dinner last week, I broached the topic, and a director at the table said that after he'd sworn off orgasms, he'd done the best work of his career.

As one of my editors used to tell me, it takes three to make an argument. So these three people, all far more successful than I am—combined with lingering adolescent self-flagellation guilt—inspired the 30 Day Experiment: No ejaculation for a month.

And today has been torture. Women I'm either sleeping with or want to sleep with have been calling nonstop. Then, worst of all, Kimberly decides to graduate from text sex to phone sex.

While we're talking about the Russian director Timur Bek-mambetov, she starts breathing heavily into the phone.

"What are you doing right now?" I ask.

"I'm rubbing the outside of my panties." Her voice alone—candied, coy, and playful—turns me on. From the moment she said "hi," I was as hard as a crowbar—it doesn't take much these days. Now the pressure is too much to bear.

Rather than talking dirty to me, she just moans into the phone as she touches herself. This is actually hotter than ordinary phone sex because it seems more like we're doing it instead of just discussing it.

I bring myself dangerously close to the brink, then stop and take deep, calming breaths. I begin again, as she moans louder and sharper, breathes faster and shorter. I want her so badly. It feels as if there's a cord of sexual energy shooting from my body all the way to her in New York. I've never experienced anything like this during phone sex, probably because in the past I was too busy working toward my own orgasm.

After a few cycles of pleasure and denial, something else I've never experienced happens: my inner thighs and stomach—just above and below the crotch—begin tingling intensely. They feel simultaneously warm and cold, like they're covered with those icy-hot creams people use for pain relief.

"Did you come?" Kimberly asks after her orgasm subsides.

"I can't."

"What do you mean?" She sounds concerned.

I hesitate for a moment, then decide to risk explaining the 30 Day Experiment. There is silence on her end. She probably thinks I'm a freak.

"I want you to come," she pleads. "It makes me feel inadequate, like I wasn't good enough."

"You were so hot," I tell her. "I've never been that turned on over the phone."

She hangs up, dejected. I've tampered with the natural order of things. Women are so conditioned to expect a guy to come that when he doesn't, even if she has an orgasm, they tend to feel like the sex was incomplete.

I haven't met this girl yet and I'm already destroying her self-esteem.

Two hours later, my thighs and stomach a feel like cold needles stuck into hot skin.

THE FOURTH DAY

Twelve times twelve is 144.

Eighteen times eighteen is 324.

Twenty-three times twenty-three is 529.

I can multiply any two numbers up to twenty-five together in an instant. I've become like a human calculator. It's an unintended benefit of the 30 Day Experiment.

Sex with Crystal isn't easy. After a while, even doing times tables in my head is no longer enough to hold back the tides of pleasure. I make her stop when she's on the brink of orgasm because I'm right there, too. She is not happy with this.

"Don't you enjoy orgasms?" she asks.

"I love to orgasm. It's like Nature's own heroin. That's why I want to see if I can kick it."

I now know how junkies feel. There is hardly a moment that goes by that you don't think about the rush. Every cell in your body screams for it. And the longer you have to go without it, the more consuming the desire for it becomes, until it drowns every other thought.

I suppose this is the other reason I'm doing the Experiment.

I've been around some of the worst junkies in rock 'n' roll, yet I've never been addicted to anything: not even coffee or cigarettes. I used to tell myself this was because I didn't have an addictive personality.

On further reflection, however, I realized that I was addicted to one thing. Whether with a woman or alone, I'd had at least one orgasm a day for as long as I could remember.

To make matters worse, like most addicts, I've always been plagued by guilt about my habit. As a teenager, I used to think men were allotted only a few thousand ejaculations in a lifetime and I worried that I was using up my reserve too quickly. In college, every time I came, I thought it was somehow depleting my life force. And since then, whenever I masturbate, I feel not only dirty, but that it lessens my attractiveness and desirability when I interact with women over the course of the day.

The 30 Day Experiment, then, was not an option. It was a necessity. I needed to find out if I had the strength and willpower to break this addiction—and dispel the guilt-generated superstitions I'd been nurturing since puberty.

Of course, the Experiment would be much easier without all the sex, but by learning to enjoy the journey more than the destination, I'm becoming much better in bed. At least, I think I am.

"You suck." Crystal punches me playfully in the chest and dismounts. "I didn't get to finish."

"Maybe you're too orgasm dependent," I tell her.

Crystal is a six-foot-tall psychology student who used to pressure me to be her boyfriend. When I told her I didn't feel as strongly about her, she stopped sleeping with me for her own emotional health.

A month later, she changed her mind. "I decided you're too good not to share," she explained. The next week, I introduced her to Susanna and she had her first threesome. Since then, she's been willing to try anything once.

"I want to hear more about the orgasm thing and understand what you're trying to achieve," she says as I run to the refrigerator for water, enjoying yet another benefit of the 30 Day Experiment: no more rolling over and going to sleep. Sex now energizes rather than depletes.

I explain the rationale behind the Experiment to Crystal. She considers it for a moment, then asks, "Can women do this?"

THE FIFTH DAY

Kimberly is slowly taking the place of masturbation in my life. Every day, I look more forward to our bedtime conversations. Today, she confesses her feelings for me, and I'm not even scared. "I want to know you inside and out," she says. "I want to see a picture or a shirt or a toothbrush and know it's yours. I really, really care about you and what happens to you and how you feel."

I tell her that I have to speak at a seminar in New York in six days and am extending the trip to spend more time with her. We imagine every detail of our first night together, until she comes screaming my name. It is a sound that strikes me more profoundly than the greatest symphony or the most musical bird or the noise Windows makes when loading.

Afterward, I reach a new threshold of discomfort. The triangular area of flesh just above my dick feels tender and sore. And it is nearly impossible to take a shit, because when I squeeze my muscles, unbelievable bolts of pain shoot through the area above my crotch. When I look at the skin there, it seems swollen. But then again, I don't look at it that often, so maybe it's always like that.

It is now glaringly obvious that I'm doing this wrong. Something supposedly beneficial shouldn't hurt so much. In one of my favorite self-improvement books, *Mastering Your Hidden Self*, the author, Serge Kahili King, says that quitting a habit takes more than willpower. When you stop doing something, he explains, it leaves a subconscious void. And this void must be replaced by a new activity. This is why people who quit smoking cigarettes, for example, chew gum instead.

But I can't think of any type of gum—even Freshen Up—powerful enough to take away the urgency and pain I feel. The new habit would have to be something more physical, preferably an activity that alleviates the ache, like bathing my balls in cold sour cream.

I drift off to sleep, praying for a wet dream to relieve my burden. I've never had one before, probably on account of my compulsive masturbation. I'm awakened, however, by the phone.

"I want to do it with you." It's Crystal.

"Now?" I ask, horrified perhaps for the first time in my life by the prospect of a booty call.

"No, silly. I want to do the 30 Day Experiment."

I'm happy to have a female partner in restraint. I tell her about looking for a replacement habit and we decide on something constructive: exercise.

So, for the next twenty-five days, whenever I'm aroused, I'm going to do push-ups instead of masturbating. And I will master my hidden self.

THE SIXTH DAY

I'm getting turned on by everyone and everything. The words "polymorphously perverse" come to mind for the first time since college.

I spend twenty minutes scrolling through the numbers in my phone, thinking about women I've never even found attractive. I want to send them dirty texts and tell them to come over.

I hit the floor and do thirty push-ups. The blood begins to circulate through my body instead of amassing in just one place.

Later in the day, while I'm watching *South Park* on Comedy Central, an advertisement for *Girls Gone Wild* flashes across the screen. This is my first exposure to anything even resembling porn during the Experiment, and, in my weakened state, the montage of censored breasts and college girls making out seems like the greatest filmed entertainment our culture has ever produced.

I press the back button on the TiVo, and watch the commercial again, pausing to admire a few choice Mardi Gras revelers. As my hand slips under my belt, I have an epiphany: When I touch myself but don't ejaculate, I don't feel guilty or unclean. This means that I never had masturbation guilt; it was ejaculation guilt the whole time. And this makes sense. The trope that every sperm is sacred is hammered into childrens' heads, by everything from the Bible to Monty Python. Even in the second century, the philosopher Clement of Alexandria warned would-be auto-eroticists, "Because of its divine institution for the propagation of man, the seed is not to be vainly ejaculated, nor is it to be damaged, nor is it to be wasted."

So I'm not crazy: By wasting a load of sperm, I'm harming the future of my species. Or maybe I'm helping it. Depends on who you ask.

Thirty push-ups.

South Park is back on and I'm safe. The kids are on a road trip with Cartman's mother. And Cartman is calling his mom a slut and a whore.

I look at her, all crudely drawn circles and rectangles, and think that it would be awesome to sleep with her.

My hand is down my pants. I think I'm losing it: I'm getting turned on by Cartman's mom, or at least the demographic of desperate housewives that she represents.

Thirty push-ups. I'm going to be buff in no time.

Then Kimberly calls. She is drunk. She says she misses me. I miss her, too, and we've never even met. We have phone sex until every nerve in my body is tense and ready to explode. I start imagining what it would be like to pull out of her and just spray all over like a tube of toothpaste hit by a hammer.

I apologize for the simile. But I keep teasing my body and it's taking its revenge on my mind.

More push-ups. Until I can't do any more.

I can't go on like this.

Perhaps it's not enough to simply swap habits. The entire concept of the Experiment could be a misunderstanding of the wisdom of Rivers Cuomo. Maybe the magic energy shift happens not through refraining from shooting out a milky white fluid, but from actually being desireless. This is, after all, what most great spiritual disciplines advise. To paraphrase the Buddha, craving leads to suffering. And I am definitely suffering, which is pathetic considering that it's only been six days.

THE SEVENTH DAY

Crystal calls and updates me on her first day of self-restraint. Unlike me, she did due diligence. With Google on her side, she discovered a spiritual backbone to the Experiment that I've completely neglected—more out of laziness than ignorance.

"You're just withholding and that's not healthy," she says.

"I know. It hurts when I sit now. I'm worried that I'm going to get prostate cancer or something."

"See," she says self-righteously. "You're supposed to take the life energy and, instead of holding it back like a dam, circulate it through your body."

"And how does that work exactly?"

"It's supposed to be done with a partner," she hints.

She sends me links to Taoist and Tantric Web sites with information about sexual gurus like Mantak Chia, Stephen Chang, and Alice Bunker Stockham. From Stockham's research, I learn a new phrase: "coitus reservatus"—sex without ejaculation. From Mantak Chia, I learn that it's possible to have an orgasm without actually ejaculating. And from Stephen Chang, I learn the deer exercise, which is based on ancient Taoist monks' observations of the potent, long-living deer, specifically the way it wiggles its tail to exercise its butt muscles. The ritual is supposed to spread semen from the prostate to other parts of the body. I need to do this immediately.

I sit on the toilet with my laptop computer open at my feet and follow the directions, rubbing my hands together to generate heat, then cupping my balls. I place my other hand just below my navel and move it in slow circles. Then I switch positions and repeat. For some reason, I can't imagine a deer doing this.

For part two of the exercise, I tighten my butt muscles, imagining air being drawn up my rectum, and hold it. Then I relax and repeat. It is sort of like doing butt push-ups.

The pain persists, but now it's mingled with embarrassment. I'd rather get caught masturbating than doing butt push-ups.

Before going to sleep, I call Kimberly and attempt Mantak Chia's method of orgasm without ejaculation, hoping it will provide some relief.

When she pulls a dildo out of her bedside table and narrates its next moves in graphic detail, I can't take it anymore. I press on my perineum, tighten my PC muscle, and do a butt push-up. It just barely holds back the flood. However, I don't have a dry orgasm, either.

"Oh my God, I just came so hard, baby," Kimberly gasps. "Did you come?"

"I can't yet." All I've done is make the pain worse. Why do I keep doing this to myself?

There is silence on the other end. It is not a comfortable silence.

"I'll tell you what," I decide. "When I see you in New York in four days, I'll really come. I think it would be amazing to end this experiment with you."

"But what about the thirty days?" she asks, more relieved than concerned.

Fuck the thirty days. I am willing to fail this experiment for what may be love. In fact, any excuse to end it will suffice.

THE EIGHTH DAY

As I attempt another of Crystal's ridiculous exercises—the straw meditation, which involves imagining the orgasmic energy being sucked up my spine and into my head—I remember the night I learned to masturbate.

I was at overnight camp in Wisconsin, and for some reason I will never comprehend, the two cool kids in my cabin decided to show everyone how to beat off.

I lay in my top bunk bed and watched as Alan snuck into the counselor's area and returned with a red can of Gillette shaving foam. He stood in the center of the room in his blue camp shirt and dirty white briefs, as if performing theater in the round, and addressed the nine other pubescent boys of the Axeman 2 cabin.

"Just squirt some into your palm. Then you gotta move your hand like this." He stuffed his fist into his underpants and began the demonstration. His loyal follower, Matt, hopped off his bunk bed, squished out some shaving cream, and joined him.

We were too young to know that masturbation was supposed to be a private act, its revelation to peers punishable by mockery and ostracism. In my presexual brain, it was just another group activity, like archery or orienteering.

Hank, sickly and effeminate, rolled out of bed and distributed dollops of shaving cream to everyone else in the cabin. We all got to work.

The sight, in retrospect, was ridiculous. People often wish to be innocent again, but there is no such thing as innocence. Only ignorance. And the ignorant are not blissful; they are the butt of a joke they're not even aware of.

I didn't come, or even feel much pleasure. I don't remember if anyone else came, either, but, according to Alan, that was the goal. It was a race and, after camp ended, Hank won: He wrote me a letter, excited because he'd masturbated and "a few drops of come even came out."

Almost a year later, lying in bed at home, I began pulling at myself one night. I thought of a story a friend had told about going to the movies with a girl from school and getting a hand job. I extracted every detail from him: I'd never kissed a girl before, or even been within kissing range.

As I touched myself that night, I imagined it was me getting that hand job in the movie theater. Soon, pressure begin to build and I seemed to be separating from reality. My breath caught in my throat, my body was seized by what felt like rigor mortis, and then it happened. A small pool dribbled out of the tip. I reached over my head and turned on the reading lamp next to my bed, careful not to mess it up. Then I conducted an examination. Because of the way Hank had described his come, I thought it would be clear, like raindrops. But instead it was a little viscous puddle with swirls of cloudy white and a few transparent patches.

As I write this, I realize for the first time why my sexual fantasy is fooling around in public places like clubs, theaters, and parties, where no one can see what's going on, since that's the image to which I had my first orgasm.

"You have to check this out," I told my nine-year-old brother the next day. "Follow me."

He padded into the bathroom behind me. I stood on his toilet, dropped my shorts, and thrust my hips out so that when I came, it would dribble into the sink and not make a mess. Then I got to work.

Outside of sweat and tears, I'd never known my body to make a product that wasn't waste. I was proud. I was an adult now.

THE NINTH DAY

I wake up next to Gina. She'd stopped by after bartending the night before for a quickie. But it was 3:00 a.m., and in addition to being tired, I was desireless. She took it personally.

"You're over this, aren't you?" she asks in the morning.

"What do you mean?" I protest, though I know full well what she means. In addition to my new effort to limit my desire, ever since I'd started talking to Kimberly, I'd grown more distant. "Is this because I didn't have sex with you? In twenty-one days, everything will be back to normal."

"It's not that. I love you, but I have to love myself enough to realize that you don't want this."

Above my bed, there's a small painting she made for me in happier times. She takes it off the wall and lays it in her lap. I watch her, sitting upright in the bed, her hands shaking as she struggles to remove the backing on the frame. The latches holding it in are too small and stubborn for her trembling hand.

She eventually clicks them open and pulls off the back of the frame. Instead of removing the painting, she takes the backing, pinches the black paper on the inside, and tears it off. Beneath, there is a hidden note she'd evidently written when she first gave me the present. I never even knew it was there.

She throws the torn backing onto my chest, then walks out of the house. I pick it up and read:

"You will be a great husband one day when you are ready and find the one. You will be an amazing father to cute intelligent baby Neils. You are going to hurt me. But I will always love you."

My face begins to swell, my eyes and nose feel warm and flushed, and suddenly tears begin leaking out.

I'm going to miss her. And I will always respect her: the picture frame gambit was the work of a true breakup artist.

THE TENTH DAY

Tomorrow, I'm finally going to see Kimberly. As my other relationships have fallen apart, she has remained loyal. I feel like we've met before, slept together before, pushed each other around in grocery carts before. There are moments when I actually think I love her, but I know it's just a combination of attraction, obsession, and curiosity. I'm sure she feels the same way about me.

That is, until she calls to tell me she has to take a last-minute job as a production assistant in Miami and won't be able to meet in New York.

"I don't have a choice," she says. There is a hostile, self-defensive tone to her voice that I've never heard before. "I really need the money. I have like thirteen dollars in the bank right now."

I'm crushed. I've been so fixated on meeting Kimberly in New York that I can't imagine being there without her. I start to tell her that.

"Don't," she snaps. "There's nothing I can do."

"I'm not upset," I say, upset. "This is just really unexpected. But it's not the end of the world. Maybe I can visit you in Miami after New York."

"I may have to disappear for a few days," she says, her anger melting into tears. "I just need to think about us."

The more we talk, the more emotional she gets. The more emotional she gets, the more she withdraws. "So you're not going to meet me in New York and you can't make a plan for Miami?" I feel like she's put a cigarette out in my heart. "I need to know that I'm going to see you."

"You're making me cry." She's yelling at me now. I'm dealing with emotions; my logic is useless, my anger counterproductive. All that's left is frustration, paranoia, and a sickness in every cell in my body that was anticipating the end of the 30 Day Experiment tomorrow and the beginning of a fairy-tale romance.

"If you have to disappear," I press, "then first give me a time when I can see you, so I have something to look forward to. Otherwise, this has all just been a fantasy relationship."

"A fantasy relationship?" Evidently, I've said the wrong thing again. "I wanted to see you so badly and you know that. I wanted to be your girlfriend." She stops sobbing, then hits me where I'm weakest. "Don't blame this on me. You're the one who's impotent on the phone."

On a more positive note, after we hang up and I collapse onto the floor of my bedroom, I realize something: My balls haven't ached all day. I seem to have made it through the pain period.

THE ELEVENTH DAY

The next afternoon, I'm in a cab to LAX to take a plane to New York. At the same time, Kimberly is in a cab to JFK to take a plane to Miami. Neither of us has slept. We spent the night arguing, showing each other our worst sides. And now we are texting each other the ugliest good-bye in the world: "Have a nice life."

On the plane, I'm a wreck. Sleepless, unshaven, blanched, I hold my head in my hands the whole ride and replay the conversation in my mind, regretting all the stupid things I said and wondering if Kimberly sabotaged the relationship on purpose. Perhaps she's scared to meet, worried that either she'll disappoint me or I'll let her down. Perhaps she never planned to meet in the first place because she has a boyfriend in Miami or is a lunatic telephone stalker or has a fake MySpace profile and actually looks like a linebacker.

None of these possibilities alleviates the heartbreak. I didn't know I could feel this way about someone I've never met.

The empty bed fills my hotel room like an accusation. I'd spent so many nights imagining lying here with Kimberly, seeing each other naked for the first time, acting out all our phone fantasies, taking a candlelit bath together, and then getting under the covers and talking until we fell asleep in each other's arms. I feel like a fool for trusting her, falling for her, spending all those hours on the phone building a future with her that she knew would never exist. At the same time, I wonder how much my infatuation with her was a result of transference from the 30 Day Experiment: replacing one addiction with another.

I decide to go to her favorite lounge in the city, Amalia, to search for someone just like her. Instead, I find Lucy, a young, thick Brazilian girl with a lisp, a too-tight black dress, and no interest in 60's garage-rock or grocery carts.

She follows me around Amalia, touching me at every opportunity. So I tell her, not really caring whether she accepts or rejects me, "We should take one of these girls home with us tonight."

It is presumptuous and I prepare for her to snap back, "Who says I'm going home with you?"

But instead, she snaps back, "We should take, like, five of them home."

"Who's your favorite?"

She points to a tall, frail girl with pale skin, long auburn hair, and a big, toothy smile.

Two hours later, my hotel bed is full. Lucy takes my computer and plays a Shakira video online. Then she rises and lisps along in perfect harmony while working her hips in slow circles. The tall girl, an off-Broadway actress named Mary, lies in bed on her stomach and watches. By the end of the dance, she's on her back and we're making out.

She gets the chills every time I kiss and bite her neck, each shiver shaking off a little more inhibition, until she tells me, "I want to see your cock."

I'm taken aback by her sudden boldness. It seems less like she's turned on and more like she's decided to play a role.

"Get naked," she orders. "I want to see it."

I play along, and within seconds I'm completely nude. They're both still wearing their dresses. Without clothes or even actual desire, I feel awkward. I miss Kimberly.

"I want to watch you fuck Lucy's tits."

Having something to do helps. Lucy joins us on the bed and removes her shirt. I kneel over her, put my dick between her breasts, squeeze them around me, and start sliding up and down. It is as unsexy as it sounds.

"I like watching you fuck her tits. I want to see you come all over her."

On that command, I lose what little arousal I was able to muster.

"There's something I should tell you," I begin.

They both tense, assuming the worst.

"No, it's not that."

After I explain the 30 Day Experiment, we start fooling around again. But it's not the same. Mary eventually gathers her clothes and leaves, and Lucy falls asleep while I'm going down on her.

It is the worst threesome ever and I don't care. I am beyond desire. But I am not beyond loneliness.

When I reach over to the nightstand to check my phone, I notice a text message from Kimberly. My heart clenches. I feel excitement, anxiety, curiosity, fear, and, when I see the message—"Are you phonable?"—relief.

Careful not to wake Lucy, who's lying naked and spread-eagled over the sheets, I slip into jeans and a T-shirt and tiptoe into the hallway. There's a window ledge next to the bank of elevators, and I perch there and call Kimberly.

"Hey," she says. I adore her voice. It is the sound of gravity sucking me into her world. I never thought I'd hear it again.

"I'm glad you texted." I want to tell her that I wish she were here, but I know it will upset her. "I'm sorry for overreacting. I just had my heart set on seeing you."

"I did, too. I really thought we would be together, like, really be together. But last night changed things. I saw another side of you."

"Yeah, I understand. I think the relationship went as far as it could go on the phone, until there was nowhere to go but down."

We spend the next hour trying to talk things back to the way they used to be. Eventually, we succeed. "I wish I could be with you right now," she whispers.

Minutes later, I'm squeezing myself through my jeans. "I'm imagining you fucking my face," she is saying. "You're just grabing my head and thrusting into my mouth, as hard as you can. And you're reaching down my back and putting a finger inside."

I'm not sure if this is even physically possible, but it's making me feel like I'm thirteen again and stealing my father's copies of *Penthouse* to read the letters. I undo the button of my jeans and reach into my pants.

I imagine the night as it should have happened. She is here, in my hotel room, pale body against the crumpled sheets, lips swollen and chin red from endless kisses, thighs wet from . . .

I hear an elevator whirring, people laughing. I don't stop. I'm half-exposed. The pressure is building, the body is separating. *Wet from* . . . This is the night I was supposed to end it all, the night of the toothpaste and the hammer. *Thighs wet from* . . .

I lower myself into her. I could stop. I should stop. I can't stop. She's coming. I'm coming.

I watch it release. It doesn't fly everywhere the way I expected and, on some level, hoped. It just flows out, into a giant pool, like the first time I ever came—except this time, instead of fantasizing about a public place, I'm actually in one.

An immense wave of relief spreads through every nerve ending, my eyes fill with tears of joy, and white fireworks explode lightly in my head.

"Did you come?" she asks.

"Yes." I already feel guilty: less for masturbating than for not even making it halfway through the 30 Day Experiment.

"I can't believe it took me so long to get you to do that." She pauses and I hear her suck in air. She's having an after-phone-sex cigarette. "You were giving me a complex. I thought: I'm no good. I'm not turning this man on, and he's giving me all these orgasms."

I suppose she needed the closure. And so did I. We basically had an entire relationship over the phone: we met, fell for each other, dated, had sex, fought, and broke up without even meeting. Tonight was just makeup sex.

It is clear that we will never meet. Like the idea that I could actually go thirty days without an orgasm, the relationship was just a pipe dream.

Before I go to sleep, I call Crystal in Los Angeles. She's handling the experiment just fine: no pain, no anxiety, no attraction to cartoon characters. But she's of a different gender, the one more likely to hurt after the orgasm than before.

I tell her about the benefits of the Experiment: I've been less tired during the day, possibly attracted more women, and definitely saved on Kleenex. Then I tell her about the downside: I failed. As she tries to console me, I realize that I actually set myself up to fail. I went on a diet, then hung out at Baskin-Robbins every day.

The Buddhists are right. Desire is my pilot. Most of each day is spent giving in to it. When I'm not fucking, I'm chasing. When

I'm not chasing, I'm fantasizing. I have had sex with tens of thousands of women in my mind. And now that the Experiment is over, they will be back. All of them. A parade of innocents. The college girl swinging her hips through the supermarket aisles. The secretary posing at the crosswalk as I drive past. The party girl making out in the hot tub on the reality show. The girls who have gone wild. Cartman's mom. Kimberly. If I can't have them in real life, I will have them in my imagination.

I am an addict.

I am a man.

RULE 11
NO MAN WINS
THE GAME ALONE

I.

Love is a velvet prison.

That's what I think when Dana rolls on top of me. Her eyes are shining, her lips smiling but not too much. She doesn't have to say it, but she does.

"I love you."

And then I feel the bars come down around me. They are only made of velvet. I have the physical strength to escape, but I don't have the emotional strength. And so this velvet is thicker than iron. At least I can bang my head against iron.

She looks at me, expectant, awaiting a reply. I can't speak it. I'm doing all I can to keep my eyes open. I want to go to sleep. I want her off me. Her emotions are now my burden. The wrong look, word, or gesture can singe her like a poker.

She lies on top of me, naked, her eyes searching for something in mine. When she doesn't find love, she will settle for hope. And so I am trapped. In this velvet prison.

II.

"If one of your skanky fucking whores calls and hangs up on me again," Jill fumed, "I will kill her."

"What are you talking about?" I never knew what sort of mood she'd be in when I walked through the door. "Who did what now?"

"One of your whores called," she yelled. "She said it was the wrong number, then she hung up."

"Did you ever stop to consider that maybe it actually was a wrong number?"

"Oh, she knew," she spat. "She knew it was me. The bitch."

I left the house, climbed into my car, and drove down the Pacific Coast Highway. I'd seen Jill work herself into such a frenzy over the skanks and whores I'd slept with in the past that her mouth would actually foam. I had to get my life back.

I used to tell girls that if relationships were a funnel, I wanted a woman who would travel with me up to the wide side. I never realized the inaccuracy of the metaphor until that drive: Funnels only go one way, toward the narrow side.

III.

You can smell Roger a block away. He sleeps in the streets of Boston and yells at lampposts. The people at a local bookstore who look after him tell me he was drafted to play major league baseball in the early seventies. One day, though, someone slipped acid in his beer as a joke. He was never the same.

Roky had a small, influential rock 'n' roll hit in the late sixties. Arrested for possession of a joint, he pled insanity to avoid a jail term. Successful, he was sent to a sanitarium, where years of electroshock and Thorazine treatments melted his mind. In 1981, he signed an affidavit stating that a Martian was in full possession of his body. At age fifty-four, a mental and physical wreck, he was put into legal custody of his younger brother.

My grandmother had a stroke when she was in her seventies. Afterward, she regressed to the age of thirty-two. She no longer recognized my brother or myself, and instead spent every day waiting by the telephone for her mother to call from the hospital. Her mother had died in the hospital forty years before.

There is just a thin string connecting each of us to reality. And my biggest fear is that one day it will snap, and I'll end up like Roger or Roky or my grandmother.

Except, unlike them, there will be no one to take care of me.

POSTFACE

"Kind of a cynical ending, don't you think?"

"I wouldn't say cynical. Maybe sad. Or afraid."

"After the way you've carried on with all these women, do you expect me to feel sorry for you or something?"

"That's the last thing I'd expect, especially from you." In the years that had passed, the scene hadn't changed. The producer, his houseboy, his dog didn't even appear to have aged. He was a creature of habit. And one of those habits was pointing out the inconsistencies in my thinking.

"So it's just about you feeling sorry for yourself then?"

"It's more about feeling confused. I wrote the stories you just read after the failure of two relationships. Afterward, I talked to hundreds of married men and women who felt unhappy or stuck. And I just want to make the right decisions in life."

"I see." The book manuscript sat on top of a blanket in his lap like an offensive drawing made by a schoolboy. "So why did your last relationships fail?"

"I guess they failed because the women developed certain behaviors that made me doubt the success of a forever-type relationship with them."

"And I suppose you didn't have anything to do with the development of these behaviors?"

I had walked him right to his moral high ground again. "Of course I did. It always takes two."

"And now you've decided to be alone and miserable forever?"

"I just tried so hard to make these relationships work."

"How exactly did you try?"

"I was honest. I was faithful. I cut off all the other women I was seeing. I didn't tell lies or carry on secret flirtations or sneak around behind their backs."

"And that's how you make a relationship succeed? By not having affairs with other women? That's like saying you learn to swim by getting in the water. It's a given." The sun began to sink beneath the ocean outside his picture window. "Did you ever stop to consider that you never really tried?"

"What do you mean?" The houseboy set a ceramic bowl of cherries in front of him, then lit a stick of nag champa incense. I was walking right into some sort of trap of his.

"You worked really hard to learn the game. You read every book there was, traveled around the world, met all the experts, and spent years making countless approaches to perfect the craft."

"I think I see what you're getting at."

"And what do you think that is?"

"That maybe I need to learn how to have a relationship in the same way I learned the game."

He slowly, triumphantly plucked a cherry off its stem. "Ultimately, you're going to have to make a choice at some point in your life. And that choice is to decide: Do you want to find a woman to spend your life with and make a family together? Or do you want to keep giving in to your impulses and continuing to have sexual adventures and relationships of varying lengths until you can't anymore?"

"Doesn't sound like much of a choice."

He popped the cherry into his mouth and sat contentedly on the sofa. I used to think that his slow gestures and exaggeratedly calm demeanor were an affectation, a sign of faux spirituality. But I'd since come to envy his stillness of mind.

"So let's say I choose to be with someone forever," I continued. "You're saying that I need to make that relationship a project and devote the energy I once used chasing women to getting better at it."

"Yes."

"Yes and?" He was holding out on me.

"And the challenge is to find someone to love who not only loves you in return but is also willing to work with you on this life project."

"That's easier said than done. How do you know when you've found the right person?"

"When you're with someone you grow closer to over time instead of apart from," he said. "A lot of people make the mistake of trying to defend principles in relationships. My goal is long-term happiness. And I make choices that aren't going to undermine that goal. Even if it means giving up a freedom in exchange."

"Man, that's scary." I hated that he was winning. I hated that the answer had the word *work* in it. I hated the idea of making a decision that closed other doors of possibility and experience behind it.

"Or exciting. As with learning anything, it will be difficult and there will be obstacles, but eventually you'll master it. And you'll find a strength and confidence that no amount of one-night stands and threesomes can ever give you."

"That all may be true, but there's still one problem we haven't solved." He listened intently. Solving problems was his specialty. "So what happens a few years into the relationship if I feel the call of the wild and just want to go have sex with someone new? How do I control that, or not resent her for keeping me from those experiences?"

"Well," he said patiently, "you think about how that would affect the project you've dedicated your life to. People who work in banks generally don't steal the cash. Although they want more money in the moment, they value their future more."

In the intervening years, I had interrogated many men in long-term relationships. Most of them simply gave in to the call of the wild and slept with other women behind their partner's back. But that is a recipe for disaster. Even if she never finds out, the guilt, secrecy, lying, and sneaking around eventually destroy the love a couple once had. An honest alternative is an open relationship. However, the couples I met in open relationships not only still had drama, but were no longer in love. They were just codependent.

But there are other options. "I suppose if I still wanted to have my cake and eat it, I could explore swinging or polyamory or being with a bisexual girl."

"If she's comfortable with that, I suppose it's something you could try." He paused and stroked his chin. I saw a glint in his eyes. "But there's something you need to know first."

"What's that?"

"When I was reading over that discussion of ours, I realized something." He took a sip of water. I knew that it wasn't due to thirst, but a sense of confidence that his next words would reveal my complete idiocy. "That whole idea of not having your cake and eating it—the expression is wrong. The saying should be: you can't eat your cake and have it."

"I'm not sure I get the meaning."

"It means you should be glad you were lucky enough to experience the luxury of a cake in the first place. So stop staring at it and worrying about what you'll lose by committing to it—and start enjoying it. Cakes were meant to be eaten, not collected."

I hated him sometimes. For being right.

NEIL STRAUSS is the author of the *New York Times* bestseller *The Game*. He is also the coauthor of three *New York Times* bestsellers—Jenna Jameson's *How to Make Love Like a Porn Star*, Mötley Crüe's *The Dirt,* and Marilyn Manson's *The Long Hard Road Out of Hell*—as well as Dave Navarro's *Don't Try This at Home*, a *Los Angeles Times* bestseller. A writer for *Rolling Stone*, Strauss lives in Los Angeles and can be found at www.neilstrauss .com.